The Afterlife Experience

D0921018

Other Books by the Author

Dirt, Truth, Music, and Bungee Cords: Conversations with the Souls Who Guide My Life (CreateSpace, 2015)

Soul Sins and Regrettable Lies (CreateSpace, 2016)

Soul Mechanics: Unlocking the Human Warrior (CreateSpace, 2017)

Soul Imprints: The Legacy of Existence (CreateSpace, 2018)

Soul Afterlife: Beyond the Near-Death Experience (Kindle Direct Publishing, 2020)

The Afterlife Experience

How Our Association with Nature's Elements Shapes the Outcome

Bud Megargee

Kindle Direct Publishing

Published by KDP—Kindle Direct Publishing

Contents

Author's Note

There are two principal issues to discuss before we start. I need to put into proper context why I continually find myself writing about the world of souls and, more importantly, what you are about to read: *The Afterlife Experience: How Our Association with Nature's Elements Shapes the Outcome.*

First, I never intended to write about an unconventional journey into the world of souls. Privately, I would tell friends and family that I was simply sorting through a few intimate personal and professional issues, and journaling helped me understand my life questions. In truth, I was attempting to balance several random spiritual moments that refused any form of resolution. In writing about them, I found relief.

Second, exploring the unseen world of souls was like opening a door to an unexpected form of consciousness. Unfortunately, I was quick to learn that freshly acquired open-mindedness was only the introduction to a spiritual journey. As I progressed, the shifting currents of my adventure became more than I could have imagined.

In the beginning, I was trying to show what an edgy, competitive, stubborn author could contribute to an unconventional topic: the world of souls. There was a sense that I was perfectly capable of navigating this brave new world—a universe composed of unforeseen energies and dreamlike secrets. What I was unprepared for, however, was how such a voyage would change the way I think about the everyday world in which I live.

Here is an example of what I am talking about. At times, I find myself set adrift in a series of chaotic life outbursts. These awkward moments have the capacity to stop any thoughtful life plan. They tend to fill my thoughts with a recognition of emptiness that forces me to look for what exists beyond what I experience.

There are stretches, however, when I can grasp these unusual energies. During those moments, I find myself asking questions: Why do most of us continually endure so many moments of self-doubt and confusion? The intensity we feel—is it nature's planetary story inflamed for rare occasions, or is it purposely designed?

I believe the key to human curiosity is having the ability to silently pause and think about the secrets that torment us. In these solitary instants, the broken emotional energy we feel may require that we shadow nature's truths and ask simple questions: Do nature and its elements participate in this madness? Do they encourage these happenings, or is it merely a dance we create through our thoughts and actions?

One theme that is universal throughout my previous spiritual narratives is the storybook framework and collaboration of all energy. Within the limits of my initial writings—*Soul Sins, Soul Mechanics, Soul Imprints,* and *Soul Afterlife*—there is a connection of energy with the natural elements. Ironically, this fitting together of energy may play a role in outlining how we will navigate the wealth of afterlife opportunities that exist.

In the end, however, it is our stockpiled human energy that defines all outcomes—individually, ecologically, or within the intimate fabric of our human social order. As a result, in *The Afterlife Experience,* I have chosen to examine the spiritual explanation of how the roles of water, air, fire, and earth affect what rests beyond this life.

What follows is the intentional submerging of mystical narratives in the turbulence created by positive and negative energies that are attached to nature's elements. Not everything we experience is exclusively tilted toward disorder, but we need to find our equilibrium. And the prerequisite to achieving that balance rests in answering this question: Do any of us possess the ability to identify the required energy necessary to set the scales within nature's basic elements? If so, we can ensure that all of us can live in a sensible world. *The Afterlife Experience: How Our Association with Nature's Elements Shapes the Outcome* is just such an undertaking.

Introduction

Look deep into nature, and then you will understand everything better.

— Albert Einstein

This may be difficult to say, but I have never known a day that has not been altered and sewn back together that fully represented who I am. And the reason for making that comment? Every day I have moments that are packed with uninvited, chaotic energies. It is during these challenging times that I resign myself to a protective emotional defense, especially with the goings-on I do not like or respect.

I believe that, in many ways, this daily turmoil is self-stimulated. Let me be clear: at some level, I know that life's chaotic energies can produce characterizations that are not real. I fear that, if unclouded by what is masked by habit and bias, moments of personal confusion reveal the truth of who I have become and how I think. In an offbeat way, living in a world of chaos camouflages my actions and, in the process, protects my preferred self-image.

In troubled times like these, for some unknown reason, I have the urgency to understand both myself and the world that surrounds me. I have so many questions, and I am consistently challenged because these issues tug at me during the night. They are both consciously and unconsciously relentless. And at the top of my list is this: I am not alone with these mental uncertainties. I suspect that all of us are guilty of improperly administering these emotional energies. If accurate, that might explain why we have moments of unimaginable mayhem ending in repeated episodes of reckless decision-making.

Recently, I have been preoccupied with this thought: Whatever confusion all of us experience, whatever doubts or anxieties that may arrive from our jumbled condition, why are we so easily misguided?

I would like to believe that all of us have the resources necessary to understand our unsettled, chaotic moments. That our core philosophical beliefs instinctively contribute and adjust our view of reality. Unfortunately, with the negative energies involved with our shared partisan events, what we may be missing is the proper acknowledgment that there might be more at play than we can imagine.

This is what I hope for in writing *The Afterlife Experience*: to openly and with fresh awareness review and determine the truth about our current human and spiritual condition. To unearth selected life uncertainties, for instance, are there unanticipated dynamics that ceremoniously circumvent the rudimentary energies that surround us and the way we act out our lives?

There are no universal answers to life's challenges. However, there may be untainted alternative views that have yet to be found. I would like to think that is possible. That a fresh attentiveness to the energies that surround us can attach importance to brilliant human conditions that ease our everyday insecurities.

Throughout my mystical adventures, I have traveled to the rural, mountainous regions of Pennsylvania to meet with the respected oracle Shirlet Enama. My intent? To secure an understanding bodyguard while I journey through the chaotic energies that affect a soul's after-life. I am comfortable with that approach and hope, by channeling my personal guide, Laz, I may experience alternative viewpoints on life's energy and how it is interspersed with the basic elements of nature.

Two final comments are in order before I begin. First, in what follows, I have at times changed or removed the names of people who have shared critical moments with me. Unless they gave me permission to use their names or the location of events, I chose to protect their privacy. Finally, I caution readers that these Socratic dialogues are not intended to demean or undermine any person's beliefs, religious or otherwise. They are meant only to catalog my personal journey of spiritual self-discovery. There are many paths to the truth—this is merely a continuation of mine.

Chapter 1

Rogue Souls

It would be amazing if I could find a way to become brave, curious, and gentle, like a child's adventurous wisdom. But I am not like that. I am entangled with a series of life stories that make it hard to recognize that type of innocent awareness. Here is another way to interpret what I am saying: whenever I attempt to break the mold of my human conditioning, it becomes a challenge to hold both my relative and absolute perspectives of life together at the same time. The result? A series of repetitive episodes of unwanted personal chaos emerges—the need-to-know what truths are obscured by the preconceived notions of myself, the world I inhabit, and what may lie beyond this life.

I trust I have a soul—that is naturally active with all forms of energy —yet that thought is rarely active in my head. As a result, I feel a need to examine the contrast between the obvious essential energy interactions of life and how I experience my personal chaotic moments. In doing so, I might be able to identify a balanced reason for how unanticipated negative life energies will affect an afterlife experience.

Additionally, while studying the existence of rebellious energies, I come away with two questions. First, do advanced forces have intentional designs on the disruption of life events, the objectives of which are unknown? Or am I simply unable to see what alternatives exist to counterbalance those aftereffects?

I am looking for some insight from my personal soul guide, Laz, as this voyage starts: a direction whereby I can build a foundation for further understanding of why I exist in an environment requiring the navigation of multiple instants of positive and negative confusion. What is the true purpose behind that, and how will that play out down the road?

Laz: Before we start talking about chaotic energy, I would like you to do something for me. I want you to stop for a minute and look around. People need to be more acutely aware of what is going on. I am not talking about anything clinical or a made-up conception. I am talking about what is happening with the energy on your planet.

I would like to start now because learning about the accumulation of negative energy is essential to curtailing it.

This might seem like an odd starting point, but for now, please tell me, what is your understanding of the qualities of water?

Bud: *Odd* might be an understatement regarding your first question, yet you have historically stated that water represents life. I also know that it has electrical qualities. Some believe that water, in its own way, can communicate, and environmentalists believe that we seriously abuse it.

L: Go further with your last comment—what else?

B: Are you suggesting that because of our abusive nature, water can start acting differently and participate in the negative energy you are suggesting?

L: Exactly. Think about this for a moment: Do you really think your air is free of water? Every breath you take is full of water. Water is all around you—it is in the air, the plants, the trees, the earth. It makes up the largest portion of your body as well as the bodies of animals, bugs, et cetera.

Let me ask you an important question: As we have discussed in previous books that we have written together, what do you think water is planning to do right now?

B: It could be planning what it wants to do next: its karma or its revenge.

L: In a way. As a form of energy, it is recording everything that has happened to it so it can replay it—therefore, in a sense, you are right.

Think about all the hatred, violence, and personal confusion right now. Water, when it is in a bad position, loses its connection to everything. It starts to place itself into a free-fall situation

At the start of this downward spiral, water tries to hang on to its positive nature and cling to whatever helpful water droplets it can find. It tries this so that it can lift itself up and regenerate its electric qualities.

Here is my question about this dilemma: What if it cannot catch its former position, and it completely crashes? It will not be in free fall forever—it will eventually land on surfaces and start to communicate on a new vibrational level.

B: Are you suggesting that during free fall, water is changing its electrical form, and in doing so, it is initiating a newly formed, negative vibration?

L: Water is life. In many ways, it is a creator. It is needed and involved in everything. So go back to the idea that water is in this hypothetical free fall. If that position is accurate, it is possible that every electromagnetic frequency would be affected. Think about that for a minute: What do you project could happen if something like that occurred?

B: Could water choose to go rogue? Is that where you are leading me?

L: If so, predict for me how you might see it going rogue.

B: I suspect that there are many ways for that to happen. I assume it could form into catastrophic events—like floods.

L: That could certainly be part of it, but more importantly, it could start to communicate differently. Now, why would that be a problem for someone like you—or any human, for that matter?

B: Frankly, I would not know what to expect from water if those conditions existed.

L: What you are not picking up is that it is penetrating everything with this newly formed, negative rogue message because water is in everything. If that were the case, what do you think water would produce?

B: It would be directing its negative vibration into everything it touches, correct?

L: You are accurate in your assessment, but there is a bigger picture here. Let me help if I may—it will communicate its negative message with the water that makes up the human body, and if that message is extremely negative, it could shut down your biological systems.

B: That is unsettling, to say the least.

L: I do not want you to get lost in this discussion, so allow me to recap for a second. Dissenting natural elements can and have formed throughout human history. If this current human experience, which you are a part of, keeps lowering the vibrational level of this planet, I assure you that the element of water will bring its rogue vibration level into play because it can.

B: Laz, I can't think of one person who would agree, accept, or understand that this could occur in the form you are presenting it this evening.

L: You might be correct. As an example, you are not able to fully understand it yet because I am only now giving you this information—but this could happen if the levels of negativity continue.

B: Is this the theme for tonight: the effects of water within the condition of my earthly situation?

L: Interestingly, I was thinking of asking you—if not this, then what alternative theme would you suggest?

B: That is hard for me to say, now that you have introduced this topic. I might recommend that you simply continue with your observations and tie all of what you are suggesting to dissenting human souls—

those souls with the possibility of going rogue. In effect, tell me how, along with water, their energy has an impact on my earthly affairs and, subsequently, my afterlife.

L: I would agree with your suggestion because all this is avoidable.

B: For the sake of simplicity, I would like you to start with your basic perceptions of a rebellious soul. And it might help if you factor into your comments what affect the human body's energy would have, if any, on the development of existing rogue soul energy.

L: Bud, it is a total soul energy activity. Look at it from this perspective. Think of the soul going from lifetime to lifetime; it has done well in its development of positive frequencies and vibrations (what it is generating from its energy field). Suddenly, in its most recent incarnation, that soul hits a "deadbeat" human shell or body, with a brain wave on a significantly lower level of frequency. Ask yourself this question: Standing alone, could that act have catastrophic aftereffects on a soul and its eventual afterlife picture?

B: I am a little lost. Are there occasions when a soul would simply allow a lower vibration to take on a primary role in its current incarnation?

L: Not really, because most souls have worked hard to advance and raise their electromagnetic field, and they fight to avoid anything trying to ruin it.

B: I would like to propose an example and have you respond to it. On a scale where one is the lowest and ten is the highest, if a soul came to this place as a seven, and the human shell energy was pulling it down to a five, could that soul inject a strategy to stay at a level seven and save itself from going rogue?

L: Absolutely, because the lower shell vibrations directly affect the soul's energy, even though the soul's vibration was set at a seven upon incarnation. If unattended, the affected soul would simply have to start its development all over again.

Let me ask you something in return: Why do you think a soul would allow a lower vibration to overtake it and run the risk of becoming a rogue form of energy?

B: With what you are suggesting, could that soul be planning to skate through its current incarnation?

L: There are few who would make that decision.

B: Are these souls inclined to substance abuse or suicide?

L: In those cases, the shell is making those decisions, not the soul. Think of it this way: the subconscious mind is running the soul, and the brain is running the shell.

B: I am smiling because I would think that science would have a challenge believing what you just described.

L: You would be right. Researchers are seriously challenged by the entire concept of human consciousness. They are still trying to figure out how you got here and why all of you exist.

B: Can we pause for a moment because I could ask you a thousand questions about this portion of the topic. Try answering this question: Can you give me a simple profile of a rebellious soul?

L: OK. Let's examine a negative profile first because that will assist in answering the previous question as to why a soul would allow for a lower vibration and, as a result, be susceptible to the water problem we discussed at the beginning.

Assume that a negative, rebellious soul has been lowering itself throughout the years. Assume further that its negative energy is severe and that you and I would consider that extremely dangerous. This type of soul would be thriving on that lower energy.

Now, imagine that upon that soul's next incarnation, it is aligned with a highly religious family. It would do everything possible to keep itself feeding on the negative energy and, in the process, creating a living hell for the family it was delivered to. This soul likes its current lower vibration level, and it is attaching itself to the energy that will allow it to control that position. Your behaviorists would know that if the human ego desires control, it will do whatever is possible to stay in control—understand?

B: Is this intentional? What I mean to say is this: Was it a design of the soul's incarnation?

L: Not necessarily. Sometimes the joining of soul and shell is like mixing two vastly different seeds, and the result is a lowering of the energy levels.

B: The soul becomes more comfortable with the resulting level of vibration?

L: Absolutely. Think of this: what your energy gravitates toward, so goes your attention. Equally, wherever your attention goes, so goes your energy.

Regardless of the situation, the net result is a soul attaching itself to what is most comfortable for that incarnation—that is the answer to the previous question.

B: So, as an example, a soul comes into an incarnation to learn, and in the examples, you are giving, the choice is made to experience it from a negative energy perspective. Remembering our previous conversations—souls learn from both the yin and the yang of a life cycle—is all that accurate?

L: Regarding the negative profile, you now have it. Think of the number of families you have worked with over the years where the parents could not believe how their child turned out. This answers some of those questions.

B: Just to be clear, every situation you are giving may not be an intentional design of an incarnation but a modification of a soul journey once it arrived here?

L: Yes. Let me add another thing that can be possible with this soul energy: a soul can be considered "good" and doing well and growing with its energy field, and suddenly something traumatic happens to either the shell or a member of its family. That can initiate a negative vibration that supersedes the original intent of the soul's incarnation.

B: You have mentioned in the past how something innocent, like one of nature's violent storms hitting and destroying an individual's home or animals, can start that ball rolling.

Laz, I don't mean to intentionally distract you, but I need some balance here—can you shift gears momentarily and look at a positive version of what we have been discussing?

L: Again, presume that a soul has been growing positive energies throughout its most recent incarnations, and regardless of the type of shell it acquires, it makes the best of it by looking at the glass as half-full. Its singular focus is positive development and evolution. As an example, your monk friends fall into that category.

Human negative energy does not get to this soul and, as a result, never interrupts its positive energy development or momentum. It is ignoring a harmful position of the world it inhabits, and everything that is off-putting is not given a position of existence.

And the learning about everything we just discussed? The minute anyone thinks or gives energy toward a negative event, they have fueled that monster, and once that occurs, things start to fall apart.

B: You have given negative energy a life or a purpose.

L: Yes. But you know all about this. Human ego or logic goes to everything. People create their own destiny, and interestingly, most people instinctively know that.

To make it more succinct, I want to talk about the concept of "like attracts like" for a moment and its effect on a soul's rebellion. Just think for a moment: Why have you created the positions in life that you have experienced? Additionally, why would you then continue to create some of those conditions?

B: As you have laid out, is it possible that I have slid from the level of energy I brought into the incarnation?

L: Good. That would, in part, be true. Let us go further. Why would anyone, including yourself, seek to be pleased with that slippage but not concerned enough to change it?

B: I believe that I might not have accepted or been aware of things as they were obviously presented and, as a result, tumbled into negative positions. Would that be accurate?

L: Exactly, and it all goes back to the human ego's desire to control. In an interesting way, it is not completely a negative control issue. In many instances, some of you will seek to initiate control over a life event so the shell does not get emotionally hurt, thereby experiencing increasing negative feelings, leading to a lowering of its vibration.

Oddly, here is an interesting view that a rebellious soul typically maintains. Most of them tried to reactively even up the odds by initiating the karma they created rather than waiting for it to happen naturally. Or, simply put, selfishly wanting to go out on its own.

B: A rebellious soul, positive or negative, can accelerate its karma?

L: Yes.

B: And it would do that intentionally?

L: Yes.

B: I want to check something to be completely accurate: Are you suggesting that this act alone represents the power of a rebellious soul and not necessarily something the spirit world would allow?

L: Yes.

B: Laz, I would like to ask a question that has been on my mind and relates to tonight's discussion. With everything that is happening on our planet now, are we in the center of a swirling tunnel of negative energy, and might that have a damaging impact on an afterlife?

L: Yes. But let's explain all the contents of this imaginary tunnel you reference because you are in both the mix and the midst of all of it, and I would like to explain both.

The mix represents how the souls have all found one another, and that could be both on your planet and in the spirit world. Simply put, there are both positive rebellious souls working to make things better and negative rebellious souls trying to make them more chaotic. It is like they are choosing sides.

B: That is an odd comment, and because of it, I have two questions. First, are the positive rebellious souls that are joining together to assist this planet the Human Warrior souls that you have referenced in the past? Souls that are primarily responsible for balancing out energy? (see Appendix A for an explanation of a Human Warrior)

L: Most certainly they are on the front lines because they refuse to be taken over by the negative energy that is created.

B: My second question is this: Do all of us have the capacity to become or assist that group of souls, and could that present a more positive afterlife picture?

L: One hundred percent.

B: Has the situation that all of us find ourselves in—is it part of an incarnation plan initiated by all the souls on the planet at this time? Did we sign up for this and its inevitable conclusion?

L: Not exactly. It is something that all of you chose to create because you saw the need for it.

Here is how this happened. If you stare at something long enough, it becomes the center of your universe, and that is where your energy goes.

Conversely, your soul is cut like a diamond, and therefore, it can divide its energies to create multiple outcomes that involve chaotic energies. You could address the negative situation and still move to advance your positive energy to another level.

Frankly, with the level of negative energy on your planet, I am amazed at how the Human Warriors who are focused exclusively on positive energies can master any positive outcomes.

B: I am looking for something to hang my hat on this evening that would make me feel better about your discussion. Is it a matter of allocating my positive energies and addressing the concentration and focus that is necessary to create alternative outcomes in my life and the lives of those around me?

L: Of course, and with that question, we have talked enough for this evening. I will have more next time.

I will need you to think about our interactions with the natural elements that make up your world because we will be traveling that road throughout this journey. Become open-minded—it will aid you in understanding what I just laid out in front of you.

This portion of your journey—venturing into the world of rogue souls and chaotic energies—will not be easily understood. You're thinking on this will be seriously challenged.

Throughout my spiritual journey, I have traveled to Buddhist communities to seek alternative views on philosophy, consciousness, the afterlife, and useful forms of alternative medicine. On every occasion, I am greeted with an adapted form of the Latin phrase *quid petis* (what do you seek?). Ironically, I found myself asking that exact question internally following my latest dialogue with Laz.

For the record, most of my yearly monastery stopovers are not connected with the world in which I grew up. There is an out-of-date feel to these visits; although they are far removed from the world I know, they have the magical quality of separating me from the mystical challenges I face. Within cloistered environments, there is a detached view of life's confusion and uncertainty, which breeds a feeling of clarity and focused awareness. Now, as I begin the process of exploring the idea of rogue energy and how that might affect this life, I have a similar sensation—the feeling that my body is in one place while my mind is in another, struggling to filter what has been shared.

Ironically, I do not always feel fully connected to what Laz shares. I know this because I regularly struggle to understand what occurs in the world of souls. Additionally, my skeptical and unsettled personality simply continues to ask questions. As an example, when different worlds join forces, do they underline the deepening spirituality of life's unknown issues—the happenings within my life that are both indispensable and rarely recognized?

Not long ago, I had a conversation with a close friend about my most recent soul world adventure and concluded that often, the impact of new and unconventional information changes the direction of my spiritual voyage. I interpreted his comments in this fashion: when I seriously investigate what Laz shares about nature's elements, I unexpectedly find a fluidity of thought where before I would only assume permanence. In constructing an open-minded recognition of transcendent views, I no longer get carried away by the cynical stories that are introduced by others, the hoaxes that keep my mind spinning in repetitive cycles.

Obviously, I am seeking something from the sacred corners of the nonphysical world that Laz occupies. I am trusting that whatever I find will help in isolating the modern-day problems caused by jumbled life energies and set a focused course for a positive afterlife.

My concluding thoughts on tonight's discussion? These are not the best of times for many of us. The answers we seek to our lives become unclear when surrounded by cluttered, emotional instability. Tragically, if we are unable to find our solutions, the water analogy Laz shared can become an active option.

I am curious where my spiritual monk will take all this. I am hoping he will build on the power and inevitable consequences of modifying nature's rogue energy.

Chapter 2

Broken Energy

When I was twenty-two and a struggling psychology intern, my clinical mentor and tutor asked me a series of questions with the aim of removing any unwanted medical rubble I had assembled during my graduate school years. His professional intention? To challenge my thinking and gently guide me into a world of hopeful humanistic healing. His name was Anthony Crane, PhD.

Dr. Crane's administrative and clinical/supervisory approach to newly appointed clinicians was anything but mainstream. To be drawn into his clever interpretation of perplexing emotional conditions involved an intentional break from irrefutable teaching/learning styles. In many ways, it required that I take a blind professional leap of faith. Here are examples of what I am talking about.

I remember casually walking into the observation room following one of my very first clinical encounters. Dr. Crane was rewinding the videotape of my session, and without looking up, he asked a simple question: "Who do you think just walked into that room with you today?" I fumbled with the patient chart, looking for a name. Perplexed, he looked at me, shook his head, and uttered, "You have no idea why I asked that question, do you?"

To the outsider, that moment might appear simple and uncomplicated, but for me, it revealed a launching point for what would follow. Unbeknownst to me, I was meeting what my Buddhist friends would later describe as "an illuminated moment of truth"—an occasion when I needed to place more wood on the fire, the time when I am asked to break free from conventional understandings and seek alternative points of view.

Dr. Crane was not looking for a name, nor was he looking for my clinical interpretations or suggested treatment options. He wanted me to look beyond the obvious and outside my clinical and academic theories.

For the next hour, Dr. Crane focused his comments on interpretations of theoretical observations that would preoccupy my thinking for the rest of my clinical career. From those moments forward, my challenge was to uncover the planned, accidental, and complex forms of patient camouflage. I would no longer be probed solely for an analytical behavioral opinion. I would need to balance what I saw and did not see. From Dr. Crane's point of view, the personal chaos created by the modest act of attending an interview appointment had unveiled an internal emotional state, and I was merely being questioned as to which rendition of the person I had encountered.

This is my rationale for recalling this story, exposing the hidden moments that staple together the impact of chaotic life energies and explain the emotional healing exits that have been falsely sealed. In effect, they teach us how to neutralize our personal, negative, chaotic conditions—especially those we struggle to outlast.

These are unsettled times, and our lives have become analogous to a small pocket mirror crashing to the floor. At that moment, energy becomes detached and separates into multiple splintered pieces. When examined, these moments reveal a pattern of off-putting energy. Becoming intensely aware of the chaotic effects of those energies gives us the chance to put our mirror back together.

I believe my spirit friend has started to construct a platform for understanding the chaotic energy of the soul, one that starts by categorizing the natural broken vibrations of all earth's natural soul energies. Yet, at this moment, I am unsure what is next or how any of this will tie together with my potential afterlife activities. For now, I am cautiously gathering questions and holding on for the ride.

Bud: Laz, to start this evening: with the amount of negative energy that is being spread throughout the world, are we able to start making some serious, bilateral choices about how we are going to live going forward?

Laz: There will not be a choice. Previously, there might have been a bilateral choice between moving in a highly technological world or moving back to a more locally organized, simple community life, but that time has passed.

With the choice of an established technological world, the planet's inhabitants will have to live in that system, or they will be unable to exist. For example, people will not be able to buy or sell things without going with a highly advanced, high-tech life plan.

B: Then we will be moving from trying to control our internal worlds to emphasizing how we will be controlled?

L: With the broken energy and chaos that exist today, I am not sure there was ever a desire to have everyone find a more comfortable position within themselves. Just think about the amount of soul or human energy that is being affected by the substances that are available in your world: alcohol, pharmaceuticals, and so much more.

Then look at the changes in the air, the earth, the water, as well as the polarities of your planet—all this is shaping the energy of your world.

B: How does that relate to my life today?

L: A prime example is the virus you are currently trying to navigate. Let's examine this with a simple question. When a virus enters your body, what does it do?

B: Are you suggesting that it changes the level of our energy, which then makes it consistent with the jumbled energy around us?

L: It attaches to your underlying problems. Take this back to your original questions: If the energy of the soul is chaotic and layered on top of a chaotic planet, what do you think you get from that?

B: I see a questionable domino effect occurring.

L: Absolutely. Things cannot connect. For example, if you shake all ten of your fingers and try to interlock them at the same time, it is impossible. When you apply that story to your planet and its current energy, nothing is connecting in the way that was intended.

B: Laz, what has led us to this point in time?

L: It is a serious shifting of the conscious mind. Think about this: If you put ten people in a room and everybody wants one thing, but not the same thing, do you really think there will be enough solid energy to find something that everyone can agree on? Some might get bits and pieces of what they want but nothing completely satisfying. In a situation like this, you are dealing with broken energy.

B: Laz, there is an author—Edward Lorenz—who coined the term "butterfly effect" in the context of chaos theory. Meaning the movement of a butterfly can change the energy around it and therefore can affect the energy elsewhere.

L: You could apply that theory to anything, including the simple act of standing on the grass. You are affecting the energy arising from the ground and creating a wave or ripple of energy.

B: Can this energy be haphazard?

L: It would not be haphazard now; rather, it is merging with possible chaotic energies surrounding it.

Do this for a minute, Bud. Think of all the broken people on the planet and all the people you dealt with while running psychiatric hospitals. You were trying to put together broken people who had broken energy.

Now, to get to your larger issue, the planet's energy is breaking, along with the energy of its basic elements—what can come from these similar energies merging? This action and the energy associated with it will eventually mutate, and the only remaining question is what that fragmentation will look like.

B: Talk more about that, Laz, because that is why we started this discussion. Before coming here tonight, I assumed that this broken energy was simply a result of what was occurring in our political/societal systems, but you are suggesting something much more complex.

L: Humans react to what presents directly to them, and it overwhelms their energy. Here is a simple and relatable example: you are driving down the road, and there is another driver in a rage next to you. He gives you an insulting sign, and you return the gesture. So, what has this energy exchange become in one second?

B: Well, it certainly is negative, and that negativity has been imprinted or established in some fashion in that general area.

L: Yes, but it has also blended into the fabric of other localized chaotic energies.

Go back for a moment to try to fully understand this example—broken energy with broken humans on a broken planet converging with one simple gesture. It is imprinted and therefore stays and will eventually join with other broken energies, including those in nature's elements. What do you think happens to all that? Your answer: things are never going to be the same where that energy occurred.

B: Let me ask you a broader question. Is it possible that some things are so severely broken they are unfixable?

L: Absolutely. Think about a situation when serious physical altercations took place. Imagine there is one individual who sees all the damage being inflicted on the individuals in the altercation. That individual screams during it. The energy displayed by that individual is now imprinted at that site, and years later, other individuals may imagine or feel that chaotic energy through its vibration or, in extreme cases, hear the imprint. It is the broken energy around the event that allows that to occur.

B: Do I feel the energy vibration?

L: Yes, you feel the emotion of the actual event. As an example, if there were punches to the stomach during the altercation, a visitor could become slightly nauseous without realizing what had occurred when passing through the area where the chaos took place.

Now, back to the broader question you started with tonight. Think of what is going on now on your planet that is being imprinted and always playing itself out. How could it ever be considered "normal" at this point?

B: To introduce the current political example on our planet, is that broken energy simply pouring gas on our problems?

L: Yes. More than anyone knows because if it is politically introduced, that means it is set to directly control others and is being coordinated to work with the broken energy. This makes what you are referencing significantly more complex.

B: Is it a fight between what we tend to watch or listen to in our news programs?

L: No, it is a fight between every living thing on your planet. Here is an example: the deer wandering in the field is concentrating on controlling what it is to eat. Similarly, the bear is also trying to control where its next meal will come from and when. Humans try to control who they are dating, what they are eating, who they are eating with, where they work, where they live, et cetera. Oddly, they are not always successful with all that, yet everyone on your planet is trying to emphasize this type of control.

B: Is that by design?

L: Yes.

B: Intentional design?

L: Yes and no. The no would be the circumstance surrounding the energies that were imprinted on the environment that keep arising.

B: Events that happened hundreds of years ago?

L: Yes. It is the absolute ripple effect of past energy events.

B: If what you are suggesting is the ground floor of this energy chaos, then today's broken energy is an accumulation of energy events that have occurred over time.

L: Absolutely, but how you become aware of this can dictate how you respond. Seems to me that all too many of you simply go along with the flow of the moment, which breeds chaos. In many ways, it is not unlike your psychology mentor's personal awareness teachings: some of your answers lie beyond what is obvious.

B: I am concerned with what you are saying tonight. Are you indicating to me that this level of chaotic broken energy is unstoppable?

L: No.

B: I am asking that question because my concern centers on ripple after ripple affecting all human daily lives without any prior notification. That alone could be maddening. Are we looking down the barrel of having to significantly reboot our approach to all this?

L: In a way, yes. But it would just go back to what we have been discussing. People on your planet always want more than they have—that is the centerpiece of the argument. As a result, this has been set into motion; the environment now wants more than it has. Same with animals, et cetera.

Go back to our basic premise: energy always wants energy. Energy must circulate. Energy wants to form with other energy; subsequently, you are always reaching out for more. It is that simple.

B: And can I assume this concept is universal, meaning it is not just for me on this planet?

L: Correct.

B: Laz, is there another side to this we need to discuss? This part of our conversation is disheartening.

L: Yes, and it is love. People on your planet may take issue with me, but love is the one thing you cannot control. Any love that is being controlled is not real.

B: Does the love you are talking about exist—unconditionally or otherwise?

L: It is in everything—it is simply a matter of who realizes it.

B: I am confused. Does the chaotic broken energy we have been discussing overwhelm our opportunity to become aware of it?

L: Not exactly. The environment and its broken energy dictates whether you want it or not.

B: If true, then why do we lack the ability to understand the complexity of this?

L: Simply put, it is a lack of real empathy. People who know and can navigate the chaos we have been discussing have had the experience of being completely empathetic to an individual or event.

Think about this for a moment: Who really has empathy? Because from a soul perspective, which is radically different from a human view, empathy is the ability to have complete unconditional love toward everything. Unfortunately, it is not the person who had one experience of empathy for a person or an event. Unconditional love is for everything and for all creation, not just human considerations.

B: I would agree that empathy is sometimes associated with a singular event or person, not necessarily spread to all creations.

L: That makes the spiritual version of unconditional love difficult. It seems to me that the concept of empathy and subsequently the unconditional love that you should experience has been lost.

Let me explain something for you: there is a distinct difference between the empathy you try to achieve on your planet and what a soul might experience. The main contributor to the difference is the environment. And a major part of the environment that addresses this deficiency is the way the human ego affects the decisions that engage in achieving the level of empathy or unconditional love that a soul experiences.

B: Is it impossible to achieve what you are suggesting?

L: It is so vast and amazing it is hard to grasp. Think of trying to grab a star, which is how difficult it is in your environment.

Now, you might ask, can humans have small parts of empathy and unconditional love in their lives? The answer is absolutely. It would be different, however, from what you would experience as a soul. In a case that involves a soul, you would be absent from the chaos of your planet.

B: If that is correct, what is the best I could hope to achieve?

L: It would be whatever you could achieve internally in your life. As an example, how you can show unconditional love for yourself or how you could remove the chaos from your life. People often lose sight of the need to accomplish something for themselves before they can have sincere empathy for everything else in their environment.

B: Laz, these negative comments are anything but uplifting. Can we change the conversation? For a moment, can you focus on the *positive* chaotic energy that surrounds us?

L: In fact, it is all around you. Think about what occurs in nature. How tree seedlings are protected by the roots of surrounding trees so they can grow and develop. How many people are trying to make sure they have enough food to eat or don't lose their homes. That type of love is all around.

B: Are you suggesting that the challenge is to individually balance out the positive and negative?

L: It always was. The balance is always in how you perceive it because everyone has a different view of the topic.

Take, for example, what is happening to all of you on your planet recently. It is stunning and quite crazy. Everyone's perceptions are so remarkably different.

I am reluctant to bring this up, but examine for a moment your political arena. I will not get into the makeup of the individual worlds because it is not my place to do so; however, I will give you my view of the perceptions. One politician thinks something will save the world, whereas another thinks the exact same thing will destroy it. The perceptions will fuel their fire, and their unconditional love will have conditions that are not necessarily helpful—remember, unconditional love has the word *condition* in it.

B: What drives the conditions?

L: Easy—it is control. How to control, how they are being controlled, and how to balance the control.

B: It appears to me that within the current chaos, it becomes difficult to see balance.

L: That would be correct. Try to remember that this chaos and broken energy are, in part, a result of energy ripples that have been coming at you for decades.

Everything takes time; energy ripples need to travel through multiple frequencies to reach a certain point of impact. Not to make this too complex, but the wavelength of the ripple will have much to do with the inevitable impact.

B: Does the chaotic energy that is moving through time replicate itself identically?

L: Not necessarily, but the chaos does affect how your mind receives the energy, which, ironically, is dealing with its own chaos.

B: I think I have reached the point of saturation on this topic for tonight. Can we turn our attention to what needs to be discussed going forward?

L: Yes. The world of nature's elements that you live in and how broken energy and chaos affects them and, as a result, your afterlife plan.

I find it unusual that, with a specific intent, Laz introduced the biased communal disputes that outwardly occupy our existence. He always prefers to stay within the world of souls and develop an attentive form of storytelling or meaningful analogies to make his points. It appears that the chaotic energy packets that have been swirling throughout our shared environments over the past years have caught his attention. Then again, he might have simply tapped into what has caught mine.

On occasion, I take notes during my discussions with Laz and Shirlet; unfortunately, the only thing my mind inevitably creates are late-night mental imaginings. Here is an example of a perplexing Laz comment: chaotic souls attaching to a chaotic planet developing chaotic soul energy. I tried to visualize waking up to a reality in which I would have the full awareness necessary to connect the dots of what he was implying, to see the vastness of his comment. Sadly, I have not been successful in understanding the lessons from this evening.

What I do understand, however, is that all of us require a reserve of meaningful memories and experiences that are healthy and strong enough to help us through chaotic mental images. Sometimes when the confusion caused by chaos is so significant, we cannot see the wonders of life. As a result, I am cultivating this rudimentary theory: If I can become attentive to the energy distribution within the natural elements of life, can I show a course-plotting plan to continue unabated with all my life's remaining moments? Additionally, will these life flashes carry forward into an afterlife experience?

There are many instances when I consider myself a blue-collar spiritual explorer captured within the isolation and confusion of an untidy human experience. Unfortunately, if I keep my energy entangled in that story, it will be hard to recognize the familiarity needed to avoid life's broken, chaotic energies.

I have so much more to understand regarding these topics and more confusion to remove about how the elements of nature work in tandem with all other energies. My Buddhist brothers have always shown that nothing exists by itself, that we belong to all things, that we cannot cut reality into pieces. After this evening, I am searching for a way to fully welcome what they intended to teach me.

Chapter 3

Shattered Mirrors

I alone cannot change the world, but I can cast a stone across the water to create many ripples.

— Mother Teresa

Following my last discussion with Laz, I became preoccupied with the concept of energy rippling. This was not an entirely new concept to me; both Laz and I have talked about it before. What is different this time is the impact and complexity of such an energy distribution story-line on any future afterlife experience.

As an example: rarely have I associated how one drop of water quietly and calmly creates the power of motion. It starts quite small and builds its momentum into a ripple effect with an unknown eventual impact. Most times, I just watch the effect of a stone entering the water, never appreciating the anticipated results of that action—the final impact.

My historical psychology professors would define human energy ripples in an abstract fashion. They were likely to explain ripples as emotional impurities within a group—or, more precisely, as the transfer of moods among a group that is gathered for a complementary purpose. As a result, each of us creates—often without conscious intent or knowledge—concentric circles of influence that may affect others for years to come, if not generations. That is what Laz has suggested in his examples—that the energy distribution of a road-rage signal is, in turn, passed on to others, much like a ripple in a pond goes on and on, joining with other water particles, building its momentum.

I do not know if I entirely embrace the idea of a collective consciousness or communal energies having the ability to form a rippling force. That opinion would suggest an awareness of similar concepts that have intentionally manifested in different timelines and varying locations, with the specific purpose of creating a history of which I am aware. I am curious, however, whether there are unknown circumstances that cause surprising alterations—the type that are designed for self-serving purposes. If so, I am left with this question: Are these the historical energy ripples I seldom catalog or anticipate, although they may have a dramatic influence on my afterlife outcome?

One final comment following my last discussion: I have become increasingly curious as to how broken energy formed during life's chaotic moments might continue in an afterlife. This is not something that has actively or consistently entered my orbit of consideration. Yet energetic emotional upheaval, positive or negative, is certain to land somewhere. Laz proposes that one answer for the history of repeated life episodes just might be the recycling of life's energy packets initially left during previous times. I need to think more about that concept in preparing for tonight's discussion because, for now, I am having a challenging time connecting all these dots.

Laz: I would like you to think about the broken mirror you discussed in past summations. How would you put a shattered mirror back together? Better still, assuming that the frenzied time you are living in is a broken mirror, how can that chaos be managed?

Bud: From the global perspective, I have no answer for you tonight. The only thing that makes sense for me is that my mirror requires personal compassion and forgiveness to reassemble and glue the shattered particles back together. Does that make sense?

L: Actually, you have answered my question and you did it in one word: *compassion*. Further, you are correct that resolving all global chaos requires everyone's attention to their compassion, especially toward themselves. It is all about their attention to their internal energy, adjusting their frequency and vibration.

Here is an added thought: In addressing broken mirrors, can anyone modify the alignment of another's energy pattern? Sadly, the answer is no. In the end, only the individual can put their shattered mirror back together. Your responsibility is to address your distorted energy patterns before helping others.

B: Are you suggesting that is the only method to move out of a chaotic pattern and bring about a positive afterlife outcome?

L: You can always aid others, but the key is not to allow others to shatter your mirror while you are providing the assistance you just referenced.

Think about this: When someone comes at you, trying to change your opinion or energy, it is a subtle attempt to shatter your mirror. It can be like a hammer hitting glass and can only end by shattering your world and then your soul.

B: And this advice translates to everybody; would that be correct?

L: Yes. But given the current conditions, you need to wonder if any of this is possible. The world's energy is chaotic right now, and it must be difficult for many of you not to get caught up in all of that.

In situations like this, if someone becomes the voice of reason, they need to be a foundation for change and therefore need to be in complete control of their energy patterns; their mirror needs to be solid, unbroken. It is the only way for others to legitimately listen and judge whether they need to change also. Each of you needs to answer this question: Is your mirror undamaged, and are you your own voice?

B: I think so, but the truthful answer is not always.

L: Look at this through this lens. Look at your hands. Are they yours?

B: Of course.

L: You own everything about you: hands, eyes, voice, et cetera. Then why would you allow someone to dictate to you how to live, despite the chaos surrounding life?

You would not allow someone to walk into your home and do whatever they wanted or, for that matter, to your car. You are more important than any material possession. You can replace those items but not your shell or the energy within it.

B: Oddly, the analogy of the broken mirror works in discussing what I have done for a living in the field of behavioral health. In those instances, we are suggesting that others put their mirrors back together. Yet we are also inferring that internal compassion and forgiveness is needed so that when they look at that glued-shard mirror, it is internal compassion and forgiveness that allows for a clear mirror and the avoidance of continuing as a victim.

L: And where is this forgiveness expected to come from?

B: I have always assumed that is an internal process.

L: I am surprised you are not connecting the dots. All this—the adjustments, the examination of chaos, the response to human fluctuating energy patterns—originates from the frequency of the basic elements that surround your life, in particular the water we have been discussing these past few weeks.

Remember, you are mostly water. When you investigate the mirror in the analogy, what do you see? Does it reflect what you represent, much like what you would see if you investigated a pool of water? The person looking at the mirror is mostly water seeing a reflection of self that is made up of water. I find that fascinating, and your water may just be the most pivotal aspect of your future. With that in mind, let's take a further look at this element.

B: Do you want me to explore what the basic elements have created?

L: Exactly.

B: They make up everything. Is that where you want me to go with this part of the discussion?

L: Let me be more specific. When we talk about the mirror and reflection, we are really centering on the element of water. So, when someone sees their reflection, what are they really seeing?

B: The essence of who they are.

L: No. They see both what they want to see and what they do not want to see. It is another way of measuring—what is above, so it is below.

Assume that you investigate that mirror and see something you do not like. How is the water in your body and its reflection coinciding, and what are they sending back to you?

B: Am I changing the water within me when I do not like what I see?

L: Yes, but also within the reflection. You have created feedback, and assuming the water within you is powerful and the reflection is magnifying all this—making it doubly powerful—what will you have?

B: Could it be that I am projecting what I want to be?

L: It is simply that whatever you project you will eventually have for your own shell, your own soul, and your own reflection. That becomes your "second self," something I wanted to share with you tonight because this will all play out after you leave this life.

B: You will need to talk more about this because I am rolling my eyes at that comment.

L: You are creating what you are but also a second version of all that. For example, when you investigate the mirror, you see your reflection, and when it is a duality—the result of the reflection—it becomes a second self that everyone has, like a second life created on your energy field. It is another part of you that will, at times, second-guess what you are doing. It is something that is real but unnoticed.

B: Are you changing your original self?

L: Yes, into a reflective state that needs a singular consciousness to become malleable.

B: And all this can be temporary or permanent, depending on the intensity?

L: One hundred percent. So, as we go further with this discussion, think of the planet having a second self. Is it projecting goodness, something troublesome, or a condition of neutrality?

If you believe in a possible second self of the planet, you would be writing off the self that it was and the events that passed over all its years. When you think about this, can you begin to understand what you are dealing with during these troubled moments—the accumulation of energies over time?

B: One question before we try to expand on that: Does the energy generated from chaos play a dramatic role in developing a positive or negative response? Assuming, of course, that some chaos can be positive.

L: Yes.

B: Let me go back to the mirror. Doesn't everyone have moments when they pass the mirror and do not care what they see? Is it our responsibility to develop a consistency of what we see in the mirror?

L: Think about how some people might say, "He doesn't look like himself anymore." Have they innocently projected that, over time, through a second version of themselves, that image has caught hold? This could be positive at times. For example, losing a great deal of weight.

B: In an instance like this last example, the creation into an eventual solid form, is it both the stability and intensity of our thoughts that play the primary roles in that?

L: Yes. Here is something to talk about regarding the creation of a second self. Take a moment and recall the hurricanes your country experienced in 2020. You had a hurricane that came ashore in one state, and within a brief period, another came to the identical area with the same pattern.

B: That was strange. Answer this for me, even though it might be a distraction from your recent comment: What role does the other element—air—play in that example?

L: Strangely, air reads minds and knows the population's fear that another serious windstorm is coming. The combination of the two shaped another episode. Air connects to everything, including you. When the air connects to water, you have a reflective surface combining with all the thoughts of the planet; that alone is an extremely dangerous process, and a quick one.

B: Is the air drawing from the chaotic energy of every person who witnessed the first storm?

L: Apprehension is enormously powerful in your existence at present, and it is polluting the second self of everything, including your planet.

You know the earth cannot exempt itself from this phenomenon. Take, for example, the earth's seismic activity, the rumbles the planet feels both before a serious event and days after. They are by-products of the earth's second self; it is duplicating itself.

B: The aftershocks?

L: Yes. Can you see how most people do not connect with or see the creation of a second version of anything?

B: Frankly, I am having a tough time with this discussion.

L: Bud, people have a difficult if not impossible way of understanding that all thought creates solid form primarily because they believe that if they thought about it, it should have happened. All things created come over a period that is laced with consistency and focus. Your planet, the solar system, and the universe are prime examples of that thought process. Other events, like the hurricanes, happen more quickly and consistently.

Here is something for your notepad: What do you think the quickest self-duplication, or creation of a second self, is within nature?

B: I have no idea.

L: It is lightning. That is why you see one electrical strike, then another, quickly appearing in the sky. They are trying to rival each other. It is nature's element of fire not having a good relationship with air and water. Fire is having a fit.

B: Fire, as you just described it, is nature's part of a thunderstorm?

L: You have air and rain talking back, and then fire enters. It is like three people having an argument. For the duration of the storm, all three elements are constantly duplicating themselves.

B: And then the storms dissipate.

L: Obviously because nobody wins. In the end, the elements create a new energy form and spread out—they calm themselves. It is not unlike three humans becoming involved in an intense argument. Then they walk outside and start to feel better about everything.

B: I think I can make sense of that explanation.

L: Here is how it gets better and how we can get back to the influence of water. Think of every bit of water in the cells of your body being duplicated cells of existence, which is why a reflective cell in your body is a duplication of another. It is as if they were looking into the mirror we discussed earlier.

That process can create multiple cells, and that is why they duplicate themselves. It is their way of developing a second self. What you may also find interesting is this: when a cell dies, the water in it does not dissipate. It starts to create another cell.

B: Is it starting that process before the cell dies?

L: Yes, that process has started; it is coded in your DNA to do just that.

This may also confuse you further—something I left out: this process requires fire.

B: Is fire in that form the energy of the body?

L: Yes, but the cells fire energy. They need it to survive. They are electrical. So, not unlike the thunderstorm, the air, water, and fire create the cell.

B: Here is my question about this: Where does the energy come from?

L: From everything around you. The world, because all of you are energy. Imagine now the influence of the chaos we have been discussing, and I do not mean just your political energy fields. Think about how polluted air or water affects what we have been discussing. Is it possible that contamination or, more specifically, pollution can "mute" the capabilities of your cells? Could that process coat the cells and muddle the fire necessary to fully function?

B: I guess that would lead us to take care of not only the planet but also what we breathe.

L: Let's go just a little further in this discussion. Does something unjust result from coated air and water? Do these elements become unable to fire correctly and proficiently? I might suggest to you that when this process does not fire correctly, that is when you have the most dangerous basic element behavior. Every element is dependent on the others.

B: The elements are designed to integrate or properly blend into our biological systems, and, when coated or muted, that is when problems arise?

L: Actually, that is an obvious statement.

B: Are all human cells designed to be similar or interactive?

L: Yes, beyond what you currently understand.

B: What would science think about what you just described?

L: It would understand but take issue because it came from me.

B: I am done for the night. What is up for next time?

L: I would like to explore the element of fire in more detail. We need to dive deeper into the effects of the elements to fully understand its impact on the afterlife experience.

There was a lot in this discussion that was difficult for me to recognize. In searching for a mechanism to relieve my spiritual unease, I came upon a handwritten note a special friend wrote to me many years ago. It was during a period when I was perplexed over a chaotic relationship. I remember it like this: "During difficult yet thought-provoking times, keep your personal and future life views as vast as the cosmos and your actions as fine as a single grain of sand." Oddly, I am searching for those moments now.

I am finding the debate about chaotic soul energy and its effect on an afterlife challenging from several points of view. Specifically, if there is a lack of attentiveness to what Laz is skillfully characterizing, and any ill-conceived action on my part to remedy a shattered life energy could cause added spiritual harm.

Here is my thinking at this moment: I have come to appreciate that passionately weathered misinformation, when coupled with a rigid mind, is the same thing as being sucked up into a doomed life goal. During those moments, I hold on to what I know or what fits into my limited life experience. It is not unlike the misperceptions I encounter while passively seeing myself in a mirror. Sadly, they are amended images that easily distort and redirect the true perceptions of who I am and the negative energies I am trying to sidestep.

The remaining question from tonight's discussion could be summarized this way: What happens if I suddenly awaken to a reality that sets apart what I am unable to see in my personal mirror of life, and is there any carryover to an afterlife?

I would like to think I have the capacity to knowingly direct what will come next within the chaos I have amassed. Unfortunately, if I am wrong, there will be no way to sanction the offsetting faulty conclusions that have been stockpiled concerning who I have grown into or what I feel is inevitable.

As I become more aware of the world of chaotic energy, my confidence grows in accepting the unusual reality presented by Laz. This is especially true of the partisan views that were shared earlier. With my soulful friend's steadfast investigation, I can see how our social fabric is arranged by developing a bizarre form of second-self agreements—the more people who join an odd second self-consensus, the more real it becomes and the harder it is to change or dismantle it.

For some reason, Laz is directing me toward a better understanding of what has happened within the world I occupy. But I am curious as to how the basic elements of life will continue to factor into this world and what may lie beyond.

Chapter 4

Fire and January 6, 2021

Time spent in self-reflection is never wasted—it is an intimate date with yourself.

— Dr. Paul T.P. Wong

There are times when a prolonged exploration into the world of souls requires serious-minded thinking. This is one of those moments.

Following the last meeting with Laz, my emotions wandered and my thoughts became somber. For several years, I have enthusiastically journaled about the world of souls. Ironically, following every encounter, my mind is occupied with one question: What is more important, the material just shared or the method by which I received the information?

Obtaining and unearthing complicated soul world material while engaged with spiritual proxies can be an unrelenting intellectual challenge. How can anyone be certain of the authenticity or legitimacy of information that is mystical and unconventional?

Here is an example of what I mean. Up to this point. I have absorbed unusual and heretical perspectives regarding positive and negative rogue energies, the methods by which my conscious mind shifts, and the impact of the rippling effects of all energy on human life. I have even examined the life of a water droplet. At this moment in my adventure, I find myself struggling to find a proper home for all this and asking myself this basic question: Just because something is fantastic, does that mean portions of it cannot be true? And furthermore, how does any of this relate to my afterlife experiences?

As a result of this mental impasse, I found myself revisiting ancient philosophers to pivot my thinking. Specifically, I withdrew to my private writing space and revisited Plato's *Republic*. I did this because I was having second thoughts regarding my learning position with Laz, and I wanted to compare what I was learning to Plato's early dialogues.

Having been genuinely drawn to my soulful friend's narratives over the years, I saw how it routinely mirrored how Socrates would lead his apprentices to a state in which they were unconvinced by their own beliefs and arguments. The time they spent together developed into a process of questioning life's valued awareness. Repeatedly, Socrates confronted what they had habitually and innocently accepted as true. Holding tightly on to the afternoon and evening academic dialogues, each debater's life-led events mutated into a state of disorientation, something that the French philosopher Jacques Derrida would later describe as a state of aporia.

Gradually, Socrates liberated his students' thinking from what he considered to be flawed knowledge. In effect, his challenging paradoxes crystalized the false beliefs that prevented the students from seeing everything that existed beyond the obvious. His logic was formed with one straightforward assumption: establishing a state of aporia, thus allowing his debaters to see that their initial convictions involving the world they occupied were principally unusable, and they were without the necessary awareness to evoke clarity.

I do not identify Laz as a student or believer in the theories of Socrates, yet his storyline dialogues have put me in a muddled state of bewilderment. Now that I am about to seriously enter the world of life's basic elements and their impact on the hereafter, I fear my uncertainty may intensify. I need to find a balance in how my human ego administers this information. Up to this point, the world of souls sees the integrated power of nature's elements in a manner I could never have imagined. More disturbing is Laz's suggestion that I should prepare for something more unusual than what has already been presented.

———

Laz: I would like to start tonight with a little different topic and then move on to talk about the element of fire. So here is my question for you. Let me see how much you have retained from our teachings. Tell me, please, when people on your planet go into the confessional and talk to the priest about their misgivings, what is the sin they are confessing?

Bud: Tough question, but I have researched that throughout ancient times. Originally, sin was considered simply a human misstep.

L: And what else?

B: Are you thinking that it could also be a blemish attached to the human aura?

L: And?

B: I am a bit lost. Let me see. In organized religion, it has always been defined as an act against God. But you suggest there are soul sins that are different from sins discussed in a confessional setting.

L: Exactly. Wouldn't a sin be something, in effect, that consistently bothers you? And if something consistently bothers you, would that count as a sin?

B: By that definition, yes.

L: Then by the nature of this discussion, can a sin be described as something you carry around within yourself—a negative energy of sorts?

B: Following your logic, again my answer would be yes.

L: So, when you were younger, you would go into a box and ask to be forgiven for a misstep or the form of a gathered unstable energy field. How can you forgive somebody who has been exposed to a volatile energy field?

B: Are you trying to suggest that forgiveness is an internal process of finding compassion for ourselves?

L: I am not sure you are grasping this yet. If throughout the day there is an alternative energy field bouncing off you, how can you forgive that?

B: Is it a matter of counterbalancing with a positive action?

L: Rarely have I seen that happen. And when you counterbalance something, you are simply dealing with the new form of liveliness used within the counterbalance. That would simply muddy the waters.

B: If this is the case, is the clemency we receive an illusion of forgiveness?

L: You are starting to get it now. You have received forgiveness for a "sin" that is still bouncing off you. Sadly, then another chaotic energy bounces, then another—are you catching my drift?

B: Are you advocating that these are the energies that, regardless of having confessed to another for leniency, all of us will simply confront again upon passing?

L: It is interesting that you refer to dying as "passing" when what you are passing into is everything that we have just been discussing: one chaotic energy after another that the soul is stuck with.

Take a moment to digest all this and try to imagine what a soul could do to cleanse itself from this accumulation of "sin" baggage.

Let me give you a hint: it would be your will. Now, let us break down what I mean about your will.

B: I am sorry, Laz, but you will need to be clearer on this. I am getting confused as to where this is going.

L: The key to understanding this portion of our discussion is acknowledgment. It is recognition within the mind, body, and soul, not simply a mental act. Without acknowledgment, why would you even care? Sadly, most people do not fully own up to what you have referred to as their missteps.

B: What I am picking up from you is that you believe our system of forgiveness gives a false sense of acceptance for what we have done.

L: Of course. That is why you have the confession box. We all want someone to tell us that we are OK, that we are a good person.

Here is something that is extremely controversial: My father, your father, the creator of everything has not given anyone the ability to simply say that you are OK for what you have done, and as a result, your soul is now cleansed. He has instilled in you the ability to fully forgive yourself and subsequently cleanse your soul.

B: But that is not simply the ability to make a statement of forgiveness or a mental note to yourself and move on—is it?

L: Here is your analogy to understand this. When people treat sin like a paper clip, there are grave consequences. Think about this: when you see a paper clip on your writing desk, what do you think about? Most people think it is nothing big. The net result: most people think that a sin "forgiven" by another makes it no big deal.

When this happens, there is no true acknowledgment within your mind, body, and soul. There is no true connection for the disinformation and the energy that is bouncing off and mounting the chaotic energy around you. There is no true relationship. There are many souls who run their lives with this very heavy load of baggage because they have never fully understood the barriers to full acknowledgment. They think of it like they would a paper clip that is no longer useful to them.

B: To back up for a moment, the lack of full acknowledgment allows for a buildup of chaotic energy within each person?

L: It makes the chaos more powerful. It would be like little energy clouds with sharp teeth gnawing at you twenty-four seven; that is what chaotic energy does.

I find it interesting that, at the end of the day, energy is energy, and you are made of energy, so how do people feel when they are being mistreated?

B: Resentful?

L: Can the misgivings from the past start to break? People get sick because of the negative energy that surrounds them. Can people really respect or take notice of what is around them daily, whether it be positive or negative?

B: Is that a universal thought?

L: Think about what could come to all of you if people would make this simple adjustment—respecting the entirety of the energies that result from their actions. Take a guess as to what the planet would get if you could accomplish this simple task.

B: I can only assume more positive chaotic energy and respect.

L: Agreed. Now, here is where fire comes in as we continue to talk about the influence of the basic elements on this chaotic planetary state, and then we will tie this all back to the comments on sin. But first, like water, what is fire to you?

B: It is a source of energy.

L: And what is its purpose? By the look on your face, you need some help. It is consumption. Its intent is to consume things. Now, think of all the things that are taken for granted in a house, and one day there is a fire. People grab certain things, but when the fire consumes the entirety of the home, all the things that were taken for granted become important. But the fire took them. And why did it do that? The simple answer is because those things were not respected.

Think about a general fire that rages through a building and burns up everything in its sight but one or two things. Why is that?

B: Can this outcome be caused by something external to the building or home?

L: Yes. Some buildings or homes were never in a positive energy position, and they become vulnerable to all that negative energy.

B: I am confused. Are you suggesting that all things that are ignored are vulnerable?

L: Not at all. My point is how people value things in their lives once they're lost but never placed a positive value on them before that, including people. To have enjoyed them previously would have the impact of placing positive energy around them.

Fire is a regenerator; it takes things away so that new things can come. It will create a void where something can grow. How it arrives depends on the atmosphere of the planet, along with the energy and minds of the people.

B: We have had multiple fires in California this year. Can you comment on that?

L: They could have been extensively negative, especially if caused on purpose. When you have something using an element of nature against its natural will, it makes it predatory. Creating a predatory fire forms a hunter fire. Such fires take on a ravish approach to everything in their path.

B: How do you explain lightning strikes that start forest fires?

L: Somewhat the same, with this difference: they are two different energies. One is a hunter, and the second is quite different. The second will consume but burn out faster than a raging fire that is meant to hunt and prey on everything.

B: Talk more about the influence of fire.

L:I will, but briefly. I want to shift and talk about the fire within the soul. To start, all the elements of life have an electrical component, and you are consumed with a soul-generated energy that keeps you alive.

Soul energy, or fire, is always present yet at times dormant. What ignites the fire within the soul is the passion or a wave to do something, whether it be positive or negative. Unfortunately, with what you want to explore with me tonight, much of it is extremely negative.

B: Can I assume that the proliferation of current chaotic negative events and energy in my world is a direct result of your last statement?

L: Yes. And to draw you back to why I started with the forest fire examples, that is the result of starting a hunter fire within the souls of individuals—a predator, if you will. Think for a moment: What is the human rationale for people storming your government buildings, yelling profanities, and creating ill will toward others? That could be part of your answer.

Remember that when a fire is ignited and turned inward within the soul, it attracts other elements in the air that attach to others. The net result is your governmental buildings being attacked.

Individuals exposed to this type of energy exchange feel the power of the others. Whereas some individual souls may have been timid, now a fire is raging. Can you see how your situation is not unlike the forest fire examples?

What I find interesting is this: once the fire has burned out, there is the feeling that the individuals were not "themselves" and were merely "caught up" in the excitement. Almost admitting it was not them who created the chaos. They were caught up in the environment created by the fire's electromagnetic field, and it carried them forward.

B: Laz, is that where the saying "I saw red" comes from?

L: Yes. It is interesting that you mention that. Chaos of that magnitude can change the actual color of everyone's energy field.

B: Can you describe the details surrounding the igniting and the accumulation of the hunter fire that occurred recently with our political unrest?

L: Of course. First, the fire is ignited in the souls of the people and creates negative chaotic thoughts, which were the initial foundation. Those thoughts created the fire that eventually became the solid form.

Once the fire was set, it embraced similar souls. And as we have discussed, it then built upon itself—like a crescendo. The energy wanted to burn like the predator, destroying elements in its path. Sadly, that also encompassed people who died. They created what I call a white fire. Once a white fire is created, it draws in all the outside negative energies that are present.

In your human case, the prey attacked on that day, outside the law enforcement who were present, became the building itself—its furniture, windows, doors, et cetera.

What you need to know about this example, however, is that it started in the soul of the people before the event. The negative energy was deep and had been building, rippling in time.

B: Were some people pulled in for distinct reasons while others were simply bystanders?

L: The draw was like a magnet to steel; you decide for yourself.

B: Once a soul fire is elevated to the level you have been discussing, does it become unstoppable?

L: All fire will eventually burn itself out, including the soul fires we have just discussed. The outside variable is what is feeding the fire. Are there individuals stoking the energy?

B: One qualifying question before we move on: Is there always an ember burning within the soul that is ready to ignite? And wouldn't that be the fire that animates us?

L: Yes, in conjunction with all the elements of your planet because every element has portions of the others contained within it. There can also be duplicates—for example, when speaking of fire, there can be twin flames. These are not what humans have sometimes written about. Twin flames are not soul mates coming together but the positive and negative flame energies that can exist for every soul.

Think of two fires in somebody—or expand it to all the elements— two airs, two waters, et cetera. What would that be?

B: I am confused again. Are you suggesting two people, split?

L: You are right on the money. Think of the duality of the question. Imagine five out of ten people being split like I have suggested. Imagine the confusion and impact of that event.

Now, reverse and go back to your concern about the events at your Capitol Building and apply this discussion. That just might explain some of the behavior you experienced. Some created chaos and havoc; then, upon removing themselves from that emotional setting, they appeared calm and unaffected. That is exactly what happened.

Everybody is a mirror image of themselves. Most flames are held together as one force, like when you meditate, but when they are split, negative chaos arises.

B: Can you go any deeper with this idea of fire/flame within the human condition?

L: Sure. What happens when you touch a flame?

B: You are burned.

L: Why is that?

B: This is silly—you just are.

L: It is fire's way of telling you to back off. So, when somebody takes fire and uses it for evil purposes—like your California fires—the flame is being used for a negative purpose. That is why it is so angry, so all-consuming. It is a different kind of fire.

B: How does this relate to a human soul fire?

L: If somebody walked up to you and punched you, what would you be thinking?

B: Initially, I would be shocked. Then I'd think of retaliating.

L: Exactly. But if someone bumped you in an elevator and apologized, what would you do?

B: I would be irritated but forgiving.

L: Now, think of the flame/fire in you being forcefully ignited and goaded into a fight; it is like when you touch a flame. Taking this further, if someone is forcing you to do something, your internal fire is going to be ignited until it burns itself out.

Think of the comment people make when they say they are "burned out" at their job. It is, in part, the internal response of their fire; they are being forced to do something they no longer want to do.

If, on the other hand, you really enjoy your job, you are lighting the flame of passion to continue doing something you enjoy. Your fire is going to burn one way or another. It is up to you in which direction it will go.

B: Do we need to balance that out? And how does that relate to the phrase "burning the candle at both ends"?

L: Let us talk about that. Look at that as a physical picture, head at one end and feet at the other. People who do that intentionally have problems of the mind and lower extremities. I find it interesting that people with foot problems talk about having a burning sensation in their feet.

B: I have an unrelated question that I keep thinking about regarding fire. If you are presented with someone who is acting off their ignited fire, but you do not respond, does that diminish their flame level?

L: Absolutely. You do not become the hunted energy the other desires you to be.

For a moment, let us talk about the negative aspects of a forced fire.

What is an example of something undesirable that would relate to the element of fire?

B: That is an odd question. Could it be disease?

L: But what would have caused that disease?

B:I have no idea.

L: Let me help you. Although many of you have done better over time, the answer is smoking. You are inhaling the residue of fire that is being forced to do something it was never intended to do. Smoke is like the fire is breathing.

What could come from a situation where you are breathing in the portion of fire that is laced with negative/chaotic energy for having to do something that it objects to? Think about a fire burning down a house against its will—all the energy in that house is going chaotic. Nothing good comes from that type of situation.

B: Laz, I am exhausted from all this. Will we be talking more about this in the future?

L: We can talk about the earth's version of fire next if you would like so you can put together a full picture of the chaotic puzzle you are exploring with me. Imagine what can happen when the negative energies of the world become so intense that the earth's fire needs to expand.

B: In the example you are picturing, is the earth reacting to the chaos accentuated by the other elements?

L: So true. This may seem funny, but think of the earth shaking its fire to annoy the other elements—like shaking a bee's nest. It makes the water angry, and it resorts to flooding. The air makes incredible tornadoes and winds. The earth's fire is asking the rest of the elements to join the parade. In many ways it is not unlike what happened to your government building when you stop to think about it—the dominoes falling within each of the groups walking up the steps, joining the parade.

B: One last question before we stop. Does the element of fire resent its role in all this? The consumer of energy, the recycler of everything?

L: As I have stated previously, it depends on how the fire was initiated and brought into existence.

Here are my initial thoughts following an extremely complicated evening.

I was raised to understand that every person oversees their own good and bad deeds. That they have control over how they privately mold their own destiny. Further, every human being is an individual of great worth and a wealth of unselfish deeds and actions that are more complex than questionable.

It appears that a "soul aware" person who acknowledges their missteps constructively waits for the right time to manifest proper acknowledgment of their deeds. In short, they see every unfortunate endeavor as exclusively their responsibility, their karma, and not an action to be forgiven by another. The net result is the opportunity to address each action with a unique view of their compassion and newly formed awareness.

I have a Buddhist friend, Khenchen, with whom I visit on occasion. He is an abbot of a monastery of cloistered monks many miles from my home, and at times, I have sought his counsel on complex spiritual matters. Following my latest discussion with Laz, I wanted his opinion on what I had experienced.

Regarding sin, missteps, and forgiveness, my friend Khenchen believes that human sorrow is of our own making. It does not occur, nor can it be traced back to something done by an unlikely original person or event. He does not believe that a human life experience is just a one-off teaching/learning experience. Rather, it is an ongoing event meant to achieve the highest level of positive vibrational growth. Stated with emphasis, Khenchen believes that the act of another forgiving our unwanted acts represents an opening that allows missteps to dodge both spiritual and earthly consequences with unearned approval, the way one might look at a paper clip.

I find Khenchen to be calming, insightful, engaging, and always atypical in his view of world events. There appears to be little anxiety filtering through his monastery that could alter his internal view of the world. There is, however, enough to be aware of societal affairs.

Regarding the events of January 6, he shared the following:

"When a person places their hand on or in a fire, the hand will be burned, and the scars will remain no matter how hard one tries to remove them. The same can occur to those individuals who chose to walk into the fire that was set on that day in Washington, DC. Only they can deal with those scars. Only they know the beginning, middle, and end of their actions. Only they will experience the karmic outcomes of those acts upon passing."

There are many reasons chaotic energy occurs within the natural elements. Unfortunately, the reasons chaotic soul energy would consciously create a condition of white heat have yet to be figured out.

Understanding the logic of a predatory fire from a metaphysical position only leads to more questions. For example, is it unlikely that our individual unanswered questions are to be easily found? Unfortunately, such remedies lie within the shadows that are beyond the obvious, and only by altering our viewpoint and appreciating how dominoes fall together can they become a credible possibility.

Typically, Laz is metaphysical in his opinions, where my Buddhist friend is more traditionally spiritual. Both agree, however, that acknowledgment is an initial component of understanding the raging internal fires that have the potential to go rogue, as the hunter/predatory fires occupied Washington, DC, on January 6.

Together, they believe that people propelled into missteps need assistance in understanding they are responsible for their transgressions. That awareness of and full attention to one's appreciation of their actions are guideposts to removing negative karma and gaining meaningful forgiveness. Thus, a confession box in which someone seeks exoneration from another is alien to both my Buddhist and soul guide friends.

One final thought before I move on: for a second time within the borders of this spiritual journey, Laz has spoken to the issue of twin flames—an immensely popular descriptive term for a soul's ability to connect to an additional component of the same soul in an intimate or romantic fashion. His explanation is simple: the term represents what we already are—two flames of fire (positive and negative) burning together in an ongoing battle to balance our response to a human life.

Chapter 5

The Smoke Screen

In organizing my thoughts for an upcoming soul-related discussion, I found myself asking this basic question: Where is the line between what is real and what is imagined or unconventional? One might think that should be a simple question to answer. I believe most people would say that if you can see it, hear it, or touch it, it must be real. But what if by embracing this way of thinking, I am limiting my ability to look beyond what is observable and how I can view my human existence with new eyes?

My Buddhist friends often share that the story of the universe is a tale about human imagination: one with the mind-blowing capacity to take seriously the fact that the world I observe might not be all there is to see. They also suggest that, at some point, all spiritual adventures need to come to a moral reckoning with the world. I have always interpreted their position in this fashion: when I let go of my ego, I will become different, as will my opinion on both earthly and otherworldly matters. Also, if I am fortunate, I might select a path to become more courageous, and that alone may allow me to feel differently about this spiritual voyage and any potential afterlife venture.

This may seem unusual, but there are times when I view unworldly adventures through the eyes of an anthropologist. Here is my rationale for that comment. Anthropologists consistently ask one basic question: What is it like to live in someone else's world? In a way, this simple question reveals a very worthy life-led position. The answer identifies the curious ones who live among us. They are interested in what it is like to walk in another's shoes—in what it is like to be a completely understood human.

Whenever I find myself thinking about this approach to the world of souls, I wonder how an anthropologist might view the state of my current expedition. Specifically, might they express doubts regarding what it is like on the other side? Would they question the description of an unconventional world that is submitted by spiritual proxies? Would they ask question after question to get to the heart of otherworldly issues? Are they interested in the possibilities of a soul afterlife?

I am not sure that any of the answers to these questions matter at this stage, primarily because I am embracing the opinion that my soul companion has been silently orchestrating a change in my ability to absorb unusual information. From my point of view, Laz is maneuvering our discussions into a position where—hopefully—everything will become sharper and more naturally focused. I am hoping that is the case. I fear we are headed toward a reckoning in my journey—specifically, a change in how I associate with the basic elements of the world that I occupy and the influence they have on my afterlife experience.

Laz: Let me start tonight with fire and the smoke it produces. The ancients used smoke for a variety of reasons, not just for communication. They used it to seek hidden answers.

The smoke produced by a fire is only part of the answer we are seeking tonight. I am curious, however; what do you think smoke might be hiding? Everything about fire and smoke has something positive and something negative. What could all that be?

Bud: I understand that during a fire the energy from the substances being charred is released along with the smoke. Are you suggesting that as an answer?

L: No. I am looking deeper than that. I believe that fire, in a way, is telling you something.

B: The fire is mimicking me in some fashion?

L: At this point, the answer would be yes. It would be connected to your energy. The fire would show you something, and the smoke would hide something from you. Putting them both together would produce the correct answer to my original question.

B: I have no clue.

L: Here is a similar problem that may help your thinking. When there is a forest fire, it's for one of two reasons. One is that the fire knows what happened and is trying to convey that reason. The second lies in the fact that the smoke is hiding the reason. What do you make of that?

B: I have never looked at this situation as if it were a puzzle that needed to be solved.

L: To move forward, there must be a discussion about the soul of a fire—its energy. Everything has what you refer to as a soul. A soul is only made up of energy. Without energy, a soul, regardless of its form, would simply not exist.

Let's continue so that we may find our answer. Once the fire is set, it gives off a smoke that shelters the reason the fire is burning. It is burning the answer. The smoke is a shield hovering around that answer. Please try to respond to that scenario. Why would it be arranged like that?

B: I am not processing this beyond the obvious view that I have set a fire.

L: I can see that. Let me try something else, although it might confuse you even further. Not only is it hiding something about itself, but it is also hiding its origin. It has something to do with the fact that your body temperature is set at ninety-eight degrees.

B: I have a simple response but an inaccurate answer. Does it relate to the fact that I have a fire within me—my internal energy?

L: You are way off track. Let me try this basic question: Why would a fire have a temperature?

B: Could the answer be that a temperature indicates that the energy is activated?

L: If you were made of water, which you are, why would you need to heat your water to provide an acceptable temperature?

B: Does the idea of temperature provide an indicator that something might be wrong?

L: You're getting closer. You cannot know about fire unless you understand why it behaves the way it does. Please try to focus. Why would it be hiding something within the smoke?

B: I realize the smoke is camouflaging the answer, but I do not believe that is where you are going with this.

L: That would be correct. Again, what is the fire doing, and why would it be putting out smoke?

B: I am completely lost, but let me try to break this down. The fire is igniting elements that are now burning to give the energy of that substance back. I imagine this works only if the fire is doing a responsible job and not being set for evil purposes. If you added water to try to extinguish the fire, that would enhance the smoke. Am I getting closer to your answer?

L: Continue. You have a saying: "Where there is smoke, there is fire." Build from that. When a volcano erupts, why is it preceded by smoke?

B: It is giving cover to the fire?

L: In a way, yes. Think about the pressure released, but for a moment consider this: If a snake was coming after you from the right, but there was a cat on the left, who are you watching?

B: If I look at the cat, I am diverting myself from the real threat.

L: You are starting to get it; continue.

B: The smoke is denying me the opportunity to see what is really happening.

L: You are so close, but I am looking for one more step.

B: I am missing the obvious answer, which centers on the fire's intention, correct?

L: Keep going. Why would something divert your attention?

B: To avoid the truth. So, the fire is doing more than recycling the energies of the burning substances. It is igniting something different.

L: Here is your last clue. What does it need to burn?

B: The oxygen—the element of air—the fourth element.

L: Finally, you have it. The air is giving the fire the fuel to burn—the more air, the more intense the fire. Therefore, it is raising the fire's energy field, its temperature, making it more powerful.

B: That answers your question about temperature.

L: Yes. And the smoke screen is intended to divert you from what the fire is doing. The intention is to bring in as much air as it can.

Here is something to expand on the problem I am presenting you with fire. Why would the earth react to a fire as it does to a volcano?

B: Could it be that the earth is reacting to an alarm set off by fire and air?

L: In a way, but also think of this: the other elements are pulling energies out of the earth and throwing them into the air. That is your smoke screen.

B: During one act, all the players are involved.

L: Precisely. That is what I wanted you to say from the very beginning.

B: That is interesting, but it was a painful process to get to that answer.

L: Talk with me more about your feelings that all the players participate in this act.

B: Is it as simple as the element of water giving life to the entire process, much like it gives life to us?

L: Yes, but what else? Here is your question: Why is water even part of this process?

B: Because all the elements involved rise to meet with the water in the air?

L: That does not explain the reason water becomes a vital part of all this.

B: Well, without water you would not have had the smoke screen.

L: Now you have it.

B: That is fine, but why is there a need for a smoke screen?

L: Your answer is in the reasons that everyone develops smoke screens. It is like whenever you met a new therapeutic client when you were younger. You once said there were multiple representations of who that person was when first arriving. Essentially, covering up who they really were. The same holds true here.

B: I understand the diversion tactic, real or unintentional, but what is the cause?

L: Remember now, it is all the elements coming together to create that smoke screen. I am curious why you would think they would be hiding something.

B: OK, so it is something they wish to keep away from others.

L: Here is one of your problems, and it occurs consistently. You are looking for your answers while observing the problem through human eyes, the way you were taught. Try to look beyond the obvious.

B: This is a reach, but is it really demonstrating how the rest of the world is operating—one smoke screen after another?

L: That is the correct answer, and that is why all the elements are involved.

B: Yet the elements are not delineating whether something is good or bad—that we need to be more aware of the possibilities around us.

L: Here is your lesson for this evening: be careful about the words you hear because they may just be intentional diversions from what you really understand—and that can be both positive and negative. Some believe that before there was language, there was a design to instill feelings in words that would deliver certain messages—not spooky things but things that would "smoke screen" the real intention. Think about that for a minute.

B: I am not perplexed by this discussion, simply curious as to why you would start with fire-earth-air and then water to illustrate those things that are not always the way they seem, especially the words people use.

L: Because words make or break you.

B: What about the people who think a word is just a word, regardless of the intent, and not necessarily a smoke screen?

L: Sadly, that would not be entirely accurate. Here is something to think about before we adjourn tonight. What have you thought and spoken about over the last twenty-four hours? I will wait for your answer.

B: I presume not much of importance.

L: I am not trying to put you down. Just illustrating, again, that a mind that concentrates on superficial things might just be missing the real messages of life. Here is an example that will be "out there." Take the word *believe*. Now pull that word apart. In doing so, some people might misinterpret the meaning to assume your mind might not understand the real messages being delivered.

B: I feel like I am at a peculiar seminar with all this, lost as to how to represent it in a meaningful fashion. We start with fire and end with the word *interpretation*. I am done for tonight. Can we pick up next time?

L: Without question—but we are not finished with the way all this is misinterpreted.

After many meetings with my personal soul guide, I can only assume that the unusual is always to be anticipated, and if something was ever to be expected otherwise, I have no one to blame but myself.

As a result of my evening exploring the spiritual details of smoke, I have become captivated by the notion of camouflage. I cannot help but think that all of us are guilty of hiding things and that nature participates in that dance as well. I cannot help but wonder, however, if this position is the way of the world we occupy or the situation all of us have created.

I understand that it is possible to hide everything: feelings, past exploits, and, sadly, in the end, my true interior. If that comment is accurate, then in many ways, there is no way to know what about me is real. Under these conditions, the relentless camouflaging of my energy becomes so commonplace that spontaneity—my genuine reactions and innate self-confidence—has, by design, evaporated.

On the topic of my ongoing internal debate with the elements, my Tibetan friends have shared one comment: the word *gom*, translated as "to become familiar with." They use that word when discussing how the mind works, how it creates the shape of the world.

They emphasize that I do not immediately recognize the depth and clarity of nature's elements, yet I am made of everything they contain. My friend Khenchen once shared that I am akin to the blue sky, completely integrated with the wind and the energy from the sun. Sadly, despite the above-mentioned comments, the result remains the same: my ability to intimately connect to the elements of life is seriously cluttered, and up to this point, I have failed to dispose of any negative lifelong filters that resist being removed.

Chapter 6

The Planned Alliance with Nature's Elements

There are times when there are two isolated rooms in my mind: one filled with beliefs, judgments, and impressions that I appreciate, and a murky back room that is littered with nothing but faulty conclusions.

One thing buried deep within that darkened room is the opinion that my association with nature's elements has a distinct impact on my afterlife picture. That is seriously disquieting. I imagine when thinking about an afterlife, most of us are concerned with removing thoughts that conflict with personal religious beliefs than reflecting on the source of those opinions.

As for me, currently I am trying to think my way through a series of unsettling moments, wrestling with the assumption that there might be more to the connection Laz presents than I can imagine.

I have come to believe that there are four groupings in life—birth, aging, illness, and death—the collective passageways everyone faces as they move through life. What troubles me is this: as I move through these categories, I am hardly aware or flexible in interpreting what I have learned about my connection to the elements in each of the groupings.

Laz has firmly stated that he needs to dive further into the connection between my existence and the turbulence created by the chaotic energies of nature's elements. My Buddhist teachers always provided a gentle form of caution at unsettled times. Recently, they indicated that I require *drenpa*—the need to become more alert to how the development of my afterlife picture is playing out. I believe they may be right.

Bud: Before we start, I had a question posed to me this week about the number of nature's basic elements. Specifically, why not include metal as one of the basic elements? Can you weigh in on this before we start?

L: Look at it this way. If we were to put it into everything, metal would have a grounding effect on your chakra. Some metals can heighten your energy and reinforce it. As an example, gold can be very grounding to your energy field, but it can also be an accelerant to the meridian line in the human shell.

B: Yet why directly avoid any metal element?

L: Because it is part of the earth—metal is already here. The metal came from the element of earth.

B: However, the metals from the earth do have certain vibrations or frequencies that affect the human shell, correct?

L: Exactly. Every metal corresponds to the soul, but, again, it depends on which metals you are talking about.

From an analogy point of view, the fifth element, if you so desire to talk about it, would be the soul. If you brought in metal then, that would make more sense to me, and it could be spoken about as a sixth element.

Let's move on.

Here is what I want to talk about tonight: there is always something uneventful in an event.

B: OK. Last time we talked about smoke and fire. Are these the events we will be talking about?

L: Let's talk about all that first and relate it to you doing an interview on the internet. Before you get on your computer, what are you feeling?

B: An adrenaline or energy boost—excitement or nervousness.

L: Could you relate to those feelings as a source of fire within you?

B: Of course.

L: That would be your solar plexus coming up, that portion of your energy field igniting. Your soul is rising and harvesting energy.

If that is what is occurring, relate that back to the smoke screen we discussed last time. As an example, you have a fire set inside you, and you are harvesting energy, then suddenly, an adrenaline smoke screen comes up. Why does that happen?

B: Is it a hidden fear that I might not be good at what I am undertaking?

L: Exactly.

B: Could I interpret it as a false vibration?

L: Yes, you could, and that is why it is an event within something uneventful, and the smoke screen will eventually put out the fire.

B: It has the potential to put out the fire even if I am unaware of it happening?

L: Yes. And events like this are occurring in a chaotic fashion all over your planet.

B: Are you suggesting that these camouflaged events will immobilize people over time?

As an example, if I am participating in an active violent war and landing on an enemy beach, loaded with adrenaline and smoke-screened by fear, could I just collapse on the beach and become immobilized?

L: You just answered your own question. As you learned long ago, fear freezes you. Fear becomes water, not fire—that is what freezes you. So how do you connect to fire if you are in fear?

B: Having turned to water?

L: Precisely. Listen, think of all the fires being started on your planet. Not just fire but the essence of pure energy collapsed on itself, making fear to produce the freezing necessary to immobilize everyone. Think about that for a moment.

B: I am getting it. The introduction of fear introduces the water necessary to create the smoke screen. The fear of what is real. The picture is now clouded and unrecognizable from its original intent, subsequently introducing an event within an uneventful period.

L: You got it. Now, you must look at it this way: With everything you have written, has it been perceived through smoke because of the fear it creates within someone's belief system? If so, it is as if all you have presented could not exist.

B: And, if so, then you, Laz, do not exist. And there is no need to consider all that we have discussed.

L: That could be a problem. The chaos simply continues unabated. This is where we are now. If you take what is happening on your planet, the smoke screen presented by those who are igniting the fires and freezing the truth puts everyone into a state of disbelieving the truth. If you find yourself in this position, nothing can truly exist that is positive.

If you take this a bit further to a place where thought creates solid form, no truth will exist in a human mindset. So, the mindset can create an unnatural position and situation.

B: The reality of everything becomes the lie?

L: Absolutely, yet also a false truth. It depends on what is being pushed: the fire or the water. Imagine how that might play out in a soul's afterlife, if true.

B: I have a question. Because we are over seventy percent water, are we hypersensitive to freezing under fear?

L: You are more susceptible to fear, yes, but now without recognizing that you are "on the wheel" of the elements—you effectively are the fifth element, the soul. You are attached regarding which way these proceed. You mesh with all the elements. You are not a complete victim here.

B: But I may be unaware of what you are speaking about and incapable of balancing out the fire and water?

L: Your answer is always balance. Think of your earth as a soul, like you would think of yourself as your soul. Unfortunately, the elements of the earth are totally unbalanced and chaotic, so nothing is correct.

B: Is that because there is an absence of synchronization with the souls on this planet?

L: Absolutely. What is being put out right now is fear.

B: OK, if what you say is true, any clouded days that are coming can be blamed on all of us. And I assume there are not enough Human Warriors to go around to assist in the balance necessary to avoid negative chaos.

L: Yes. But you are wrong about the Warriors. There are enough to go around, but who is listening to them?

Think of this: your biblical martyrs, like Jesus Christ, were being executed and intentionally defiled of all their elements, especially water, and very few cared to stop it.

Here is something that troubles me: humans place a great deal of emphasis on the development of a precious diamond, yet the most crucial element they have is their water.

B: Yes, that is an upside-down pyramid.

L: Such a position only moves a soul toward the superficial, and in the end, it only results in the creation of additional fear, which creates irrational behavior that will be assessed in the afterlife.

B: Laz, help me understand something for a moment. You have always suggested that there are multiple versions of all creation, so there must have been multiple versions of what all of us are experiencing. If so, are there times when a better outcome was experienced—and what would the leading factors have been to make it look different and more positive?

L: The first thing would have been the destruction of what you refer to as negative communication, what you refer to as the media. It was the removal of the reporting of pain, suffering, confusion, and lies. You all absorb this reporting like a sponge, and when that happens, your thoughts, over time, begin to create a solid form of negativity. It is just like when a bee builds a honeycomb; that is exactly what negative seeds presented by the media accomplish. Once that type of seed is planted in the human brain, it obsesses over what was presented within the first twenty-four hours, and that starts the building process. Like the beehive, it is a never-ending story.

B: This is not an incredibly positive message.

L: Not so. Look for the Human Warriors who are around you.

B: To make this personal, because you are my primary guide, what can I do to have influence or to ferret out and align with the Human Warrior agenda?

L: All of you are doing what you can. However, the major thing missing is hope. Realize that everyone is not fighting their battle alone. Just as the honeycomb can be rebuilt for an accumulation of negative energy, it can also be rebuilt for positive energy—that is what is so amazing.

The validation that everyone seeks regarding this is within their grasp. Looking outside for this validation will produce only frustration and disappointment. As we discussed last time, looking in the direction of external validation is a smoke screen.

Let us go back to water for a moment. In part it puts out fire, and fire can dissipate water, all of it in a never-ending circle. Ironically, in a way, both fire and water represent life. When a fire burns through the forest and takes out everything, new life grows. Then fire and water need the earth because without the earth, what would sustain them? What would water have to nourish and fall on? What would fire have to extinguish?

Now, without air, all three would have nothing because they all need air to survive. Air is their heart. Can you see that nothing survives without the elements?

Finally, there is the relationship all this has to your soul. The planet has its own soul energy, and the souls occupying the planet are all of you. Think of a mother animal carrying its children on its back throughout the jungle. That is what this relationship is all about.

B: And sometimes the children run amuck?

L: Absolutely, and sadly enough, sometimes the children get on the mothers' nerves. In a way, it might represent the evolution of all things.

For now, I am going to leave you hanging on this topic. Next time we are together, I want to return to the excessive chaos you experience and its effect on the elements. That discussion will be much more intense.

———

With tonight's discussion, my thoughts on the elements have shifted. Instead of being overwhelmed by them, I have begun to welcome the connected lessons they offer. Whatever challenges I have in understanding this just may be lingering opportunities to cultivate a deeper level of awareness regarding how they relate to the construction of an afterlife. As my most recent learning moments are examples of the undecided change that is likely to occur without warning, I continue to suture together what Laz is sharing.

Recently, an analogy came to me while I was preparing for a telephone interview regarding unorthodox afterlife opportunities. I found myself absorbed in a cerebral experiment, where I fancied myself as an ancient truth seeker desperate to understand the complete reality of how nature's elements relate to an afterlife picture.

Ironically, these thoughts were not concerned with the physical nature of their existence but with the psychological aspects of their connectiveness to me. How I am of them, and they are of me.

I tried to imagine walking through a hallway filled with air, engaged with a thought process in which I could listen to its messages. What might I hear or experience if that were possible? How would those thoughts translate to the development of a positive yet undecided afterlife?

Is it conceivable that I would undergo a comprehensive physical reaction like the beginning of an alarm state: heart racing, hands clammy, and hair standing on end? Might I eventually physically collapse to the floor, holding my head while weighing the complexity of my connectiveness to nature's elements during this lifetime?

I am beginning to think more clearly about my association with nature's elements. In doing so, I am actively exploring the possibility of reducing the emotional discomfort that usually accompanies these evening discussions.

For now, however, this unorthodox journey continues with a focus on creation.

Chapter 7

Nature's Elements and Creation

As I previously mentioned, I have been developing a greater appreciation for what Laz has shared about the elements of nature. The reason for this? I no longer experience the initial emotional turmoil that is normally attached to our narrative discussions.

Here is something I rarely share—while planning an expedition into the world of souls, I have found that each new experience seeds a deeper understanding of unique possibilities. These are the moments when I get to explore the existence of life differently. Here is an example of what I am suggesting: intimately discussing my personal association with nature's elements is like suddenly uncovering a series of connected interactions that are finally validated after being unintentionally hidden from my view.

Oddly, I do not mean to suggest that I confront Laz's narratives as though they were secretly fortified or that I feel irritated by his assessment of my soul's condition. But I do ask myself these questions following many discussions: What is the perspective here? Am I missing something? What am I not seeing that he is relating?

If I can answer those questions, then, with ease, I can substitute my personal belief or interpretation of what has been shared and taught. In a way, I will be allowing myself the luxury of abandoning awkward feelings and subsequently discarding what is personally difficult to accept.

There are times when I can appropriately catalog alternative soul-related information by calculating its proper position relative to what I already accept as true. With the opportunity to connect nature's elements to my afterlife picture, only an ongoing extension of these narratives will tell if I am approaching such a moment.

———————

Laz: I would like to start with something that is very personal to you and explore your feelings about that matter. Begin with this: Why do you insist on continuing to live with only one kidney, having donated the other to a family member?

Bud: I am sorry, but how would any of this relate to what we have been discussing? The simple answer is that is the way things are following a medical procedure.

L: But why? Let us talk more about this because it does relate to what we have been discussing. Do you think it would be unreasonable for me to suggest that you have the power and responsibility to grow another?

B: Yes, I do. To think otherwise would be bizarre.

L: And to be considered bizarre would be upsetting? I am confused. Many components of your biological system can reproduce. How can the question of your kidney be any different?

The human shell is designed to keep you going. Personally, I am having difficulty with the concept of that being bizarre.

B: Are you suggesting that a kidney could reproduce the same way a liver can?

L: Let us talk about how the natural elements of your world can reproduce, and I will tie this back to our discussion. Can these elements be diverted by your thoughts? Is it possible that the elements that surround you will believe only in what you believe to be true? As an example, what would the elements believe if surrounded by someone who had no belief—much like you do not believe you can reproduce another kidney? What would they be doing individually?

B: I will go along with this train of thought but with some skepticism and only for a moment. I am hoping that there is some logic to where this discussion is headed.

L: Good, then start with air. What would it be doing?

B: Would the air become contaminated, and I would be breathing it in?

L: Fine. What would fire be doing?

B: I will answer this way: the fire within me, my energy, would be misfiring, hiccupping in an unpredictable fashion.

L: And water?

B: I can only assume my water would become stagnant.

L: And finally, the earth?

B: Become unstable?

L: So, are you suggesting to me that you would rather have all that taking place in your human shell—the contamination, the misfiring, and stagnation? And still consider any alternatives bizarre? If you really see life through that lens, who is the crazy one?

In an odd way, Bud, if you took that position, you would be trying to fit in with those who do not have an adventurous belief system and, in the process, close your mind to all the possibilities of life.

B: Are you seriously suggesting that by going along with the crowd, I am not standing up to my individuality, despite the unusual discussion of a kidney replacement?

L: Why do you and other humans consistently bend to the honor of others who will never consider honoring you or the opinions you have? Try to remember that the elements inside you modify themselves based on your reaction to the message you send to them. Whatever you believe in is what the universe that surrounds you will believe also.

B: Answer this for me, Laz: If I am standing in a crowd of one thousand people, and none of them believe what you just said, and I am simply in the middle countering that belief, what happens?

L: Obviously, the position you hold would become chaotic. There would be no value to you for having that position in comparison to the others. You would have to ask yourself if any person standing in that crowd would believe in an alternative position.

B: Excellent point. But I would be unable to adjust to any of the people in the crowd because of my presumptive alternative belief.

L: Correct. Primarily because you would be led by something else.

B: If the alternative is positive and not counter to a negative point of view, could we consider a substitute position by someone who is trying to change the environment for the better?

L: That person would be a Warrior, for sure. A true Human Warrior is someone who does not stand for outdated belief systems. They do not back down and always abide by what is in the best interest of the universe.

B: Help me understand this better. What are some of the things a Human Warrior needs to do to wall off distractions and get into a position where they fully believe in the capacity to, for instance, grow an organ?

L: Easy: trust themselves and change their mind.

B: Removing doubt?

L: Absolutely. Think about it: Why would it not be like that? Everything you are exposed to right now has a chaotic rhythm to it. In an environment like that, how can you come away feeling positive toward having the ability to create something extraordinary? It all boils down to honestly believing in yourself.

B: I might agree with you, especially with everything I am exposed to through today's social media.

L: Take a moment and think that through. Just stop and examine what you refer to as a TV commercial: What is the true message? Could it be you are too short, too heavy, too this, too that? How can anyone develop a positive belief in themselves with this intrusion all day long?

B: This chaotic form of conditioning quietly develops a message that we cannot do something—like grow an organ?

L: Correct. I have a tough time with this. Why would you or anyone else choose to accept such a message?

B: I believe you have often stated that it is in the absence of a consistent messaging system that someone would build a self-image to allow for new insight.

L: Stop again for a moment and rethink the elements around you and the chaos in which you reside. If you put all that together, are you surprised at the outcomes you experience? If people rarely believe in themselves, would it be logical for the elements to also be acting out of place?

B: You are right, and I would not be surprised. What I am curious about, however, is the inability of anyone to connect with anything you have shared tonight. I cannot see many connecting the energies we display directly to the elements that surround us. In an offbeat fashion, are the elements "channeling" all of us?

L: You would be so correct with that position. The thoughts are creating a solid form but not in the best interest of the universe. Surprisingly, it is not intended to be something that all of you deserve. It is simply an absence of awareness.

Answer this question: Is it possible that all this has been camouflaged to the point of being unrecognizable?

B: Is it the chaos that creates the camouflage? Is that the answer to this conundrum?

L: Oddly, during all this chaos, you are making yourself expendable. Here is an analogy to consider: assume that you desire a famous painting, and the moment you attempt to buy it, the auctioneer claims you can only have a copy of it. Does the painting have the same value to you?

B: If anything, it might be a false value.

L: Correct, you are creating a false signal within your soul's energy field, and that is the vibration coming off your aura at that moment. Why would you feed off something like that?

B: By having a copy of the painting, I would at least have something —just not the original.

L: Why not seek what you want? If you don't, hasn't your mind become your own prison in that moment?

B: With everything you are suggesting, the answer would be yes.

L: Then the remaining question is, why put yourself there? You have the inherent energy to make it different and remove the chaos that is camouflaging your honest desire.

To look at it another way, in effect, are you falsifying yourself and the others around you by agreeing to what the auctioneer suggested because that is what you have created?

Look at your life this way for just one second. How many times have you just gone along with the one thousand people in the crowd and buried your ability to reach a desired outcome? Many rationalize life in their heads by going against their harmonic energy field, so you are not alone in this.

The larger question is, with these assumptions, is the universe all of you are creating operating within these parameters?

B: If not, how is something like that corrected?

L: The simple answer is to go back to the elements. As an example, how does water correct itself after a hurricane reaches the shoreline? After the chaos, it balances itself.

B: How is it possible for someone like me to balance something like that?

L: With your thoughts and the acceptance of what you have truly been—removing the rationalization. Without this effort, you assume the position of victim. Oddly, once there, you almost never change.

B: The victimization rationalized the beliefs.

L: Now you have it. So, to bring it all back, when you get into the energy of the elements, who is the real victim? Let me answer for you— you are the victim because you have done it to yourself. You lie to yourself, hoping it can establish a foundation of self-esteem.

B: My compromising becomes so intense that a lie becomes the truth, if only in my mind?

L: Correct. Unfortunately, you have put a frequency inside your body that is not natural to the universe.

B: It is getting late, and I am keenly interested in what my alternative would be in situations such as you have created tonight.

L: Fine. The answers are always simple: believe in yourself and the universe you have grown. That is your reality. The remaining question is, how did you get to that place?

Unfortunately, I see very few who honestly believe in themselves to the point of changing what we started—the complete and total ability to modify everything around them. Bud, your takeaway from this evening is this: work hard to remove the doubt in your life.

There are occasions when I trust a reader to review what I have written immediately following an evening with Shirlet and Laz. They universally come to view the experience as a series of intentional, offbeat teaching/learning moments. As for me, I always refer to it as a Socratic experience.

Here is my rationale for the last statement. Laz is not holding back on some great revelation that would be passed on to only the best and brightest souls under his supervision. Rather, he is uniquely interested in having me explore the far-reaching complexities of this world. As an example, much like a responsible ancient teacher of the past, he focuses first on teaching basic principles before moving on to a more advanced topic. I believe this expedition—my crossing into the world of nature's elements—is a prime example of that tactic.

Laz does not discourage me from considering alternative views that could conflict with his interpretation of the creation of nature's elements and their inevitable impact on an afterlife. More accurately, in his fast-paced narratives, he presents a learning lab of thought that invites me to examine the ways in which aspects of nature's elements form in my daily life. In a curious way, he is designing an integrated plan for me to tolerate different opinions.

Ironically, as I listen to him, it often occurs to me that his rationale for tying nature's elements to a forthcoming afterlife can be summed up with a single word: boldness. Let me explain that comment further. I am speaking about the specific fearlessness that is required to be open-minded, to seek what may exist beyond life's obvious events, to face up to life's doubts and its uncertainties. To my mind, this is what being courageous is all about.

I would like to end with this: my learning from this evening is not directly aligned with the topic of creation. Rather, it is more that mystical events force me to face life's alternative experiences and launch me into unusual situations, like the dealings Laz has tossed my way. In this fashion, he is trying to convince me to be open-minded about his spiritual solutions, his desired outcome for all successful thought experiments.

Laz has suggested he would like to discuss vessels and containers; I am very curious how that might relate to the elements of life.

Chapter 8

Vessels and Containers

I have a psychologist friend who consistently refers to my spiritual voyage as the development of an unintended point of view—an unrefined awareness that is slowly being unlocked by challenging historical beliefs and cleverness. And his reason for sharing this? He is eternally fascinated by the spontaneous nature of events that emerge during the very first moments of a dialogue meeting with my soulful companion Laz.

He has also shared that, at times, my emotional landscape is so vast I am victimized by unintended self-inflicted wounds. As a result, he recommends that I need to answer one specific question to survive this expedition: What is the most important takeaway from these discussions? Is it my internal feelings on the matter at hand, or could it be absorbing the intimate connection I consistently debate regarding my association with nature's elements?

As I prepare for my next trip to northeast Pennsylvania, I wonder about all his comments. Especially this one: to manage an unintended point of view, I need to eliminate the way I currently observe the elements. Specifically, I need to adjust my uneasy feelings about how I connect to the elements and, eventually, the impact all this has on my image of an afterlife.

I am not sure that my psychologically focused friend's perception is accurate. Here is how I see it being different. Take a moment and imagine that the single ripple created by tossing a stone in the water is the entire river. As you sit and watch the movement of that ripple, become more aware of the vastness of the river that lies in front of you and how the result of that ripple will change the future of the water. Similarly, my upcoming interactions regarding the natural elements of the world are like that ripple, an ever-expanding view of what I am learning. What Laz is teaching me suggests that I need to look for all of life's connections and take the view of the entire river, not just the ripple. This debate on the elements appears to have one outcome: a refocused point of view.

My soulful monk has indicated his desire for me to learn about vessels and containers. Frankly, that is off course from our recent narratives. Hopefully, it will find its way into the afterlife puzzle.

Laz: I want to start with something different tonight. I would like you to raise your hands and look at them. Pay attention to the lines on them. What do you see when you look at the lines?

Bud: Do the lines tell a story?

L: That is not what I am looking for. Look again and tell me what you are holding.

B: I can only assume that your interest goes to my energy field.

L: If so, Bud, how would holding your energy field feel?

B: It feels light, like I am holding nothing or air.

L: That is strange because if it is like air, how would you explain something like a tornado?

B: Well, that is an accumulation of air and quite different from what I am looking at.

L: What would it take to make it look like a tornado?

B: Chaos?

L: And what would bring that?

B: If I am accurate, the development of a tornado would be the accumulation of what people are thinking and acting on—their intimate connection to the air around them that has been introduced into a chaotic air state.

L: That is correct. Now, how would you disconnect from all that? What I am asking you is, how do you protect yourself from being annihilated from the chaotic form or substance of air, or anything else for that matter?

B: This is far too complicated for me tonight. I do not have an immediate answer for you. I can only presume that it is tied to my ability to control my own energy at that moment.

L: Go on with that thought. What would that be?

B: It would have to be tied to my awareness and its attachment to other energies.

L: You are missing a crucial point. What is in the air? Water, correct? And what is in you? Also, water, correct? Wouldn't the answer you are seeking be how your element of water would be connecting to what we are examining?

B: Yes, but what does that have to do with what we have been discussing about everyday chaotic energy?

L: Let us try this again. Look at your hands. What do the lines form? Here is a way to help you understand: They are forming a network—a web, if you will. They are connecting, and if we retreat to the octopus' analogy we have historically talked about, how would the lines relate to that story? If you can figure that out, you will have your answer. (See Appendix B: The beginning of the Octopus Analogy)

B: OK, give me a minute to think this through. The analogy represents how a soul can divide its energy—as an example, various lives and plans for multiple incarnations. It is a map for how everything is connected. If I do not have the awareness of that attachment, I cannot attach to you or any other energy within the head of the octopus—my learning mates. But more importantly, I cannot connect to the element you are presenting.

L: Answer me this so that we may continue with this line of thinking: Why is there water in all your cells? Why is it there?

B: The cells cannot fire without it.

L: Correct. Now go back to the lines in your hand. What activates your life? It is the fire—your element of energy. Wouldn't it drive you and your life? Wouldn't it create the ley lines of your life? The accelerant for your life? Now, put that all together with the octopus' analogy and the element of water.

B: This might be strange, but if I do not have the proper understanding of my connection to water, am I incapable of becoming complete and having my energy fire in a productive fashion?

L: In a way, yes.

B: In multiple ways, the water, regardless of the source, is the projected avenue of life.

L: And what would be my connection within the octopus?

B: That is where I am lost. This is far too complex for me.

L: Let me try to help again. Why is a cell called a cell?

B:It is a container.

L: Correct. Think about the octopus' analogy again.

B: Are you suggesting that the octopus's head is like a cell—a simple container?

L: Yes.

B: And along with the water that is required within my human cells, my energy acts to catapult the multiple lives and incarnations of my soul as well as the other souls you watch over?

L: Yes, now you have it. The head of our octopus contains all the elements we have been discussing, and each of the soul energies. In a way, it all acts like a birth canal.

B: In that context, what would your role be as a watcher or guide?

L: I am a teacher, like a father would watch over others.

B: So, in a way, you have participated in the creation of what exists in the octopus head.

L: In an offhanded way, yes.

B: I have a very odd question for you, Laz, and I do not intend to distract from the rogue element discussions, but with everything you just stated, did you have a hand in essentially "drafting" who would occupy a position with the head of the octopus—the learning lab for new incarnations?

L: In many ways, yes.

B: And all the associated energies have a similarity of energy or purpose? And not to get lost in this, but all those energies are connected to all the elements in some forms yet are separate?

L: Yes. Now, let us back up for a moment and continue with the subject of lines. Why are there lines on the bottoms of your feet?

B: I think I have it. They describe the path taken, but more importantly, they are a connection to the earth element.

L: Correct—but why is there a connection?

B: Could it be as simple as their creating a grounding effect, and as a result, I am better able to connect to the energies of the other elements?

L: It is more that you have better access to the other elements, but you are on the right path.

To try to make more sense out of tonight's discussion, let me talk more about the cell. Why would the cell have to be a container for the energies that are within it? If everything is expected to be individualized in the world of elements, why do we need a vessel to have everything join or connect?

B: If a cell is like a soul, is splitting or separating part of the answer? Can the individual part of each element have the responsibility of separating from itself to join with other energies?

L: Go with that thought.

B: I know we are getting further into the octopus head analogy than I thought we would, but is the splitting represented like the tentacles would be with the soul? If this is true, each cell would be like a point on an incarnation tentacle.

L: And you realize that there are numerous cells in your body.

What would you be capable of if you realized that all those cells are attached to every tentacle of every incarnation? If anyone had that awareness, imagine what you would be capable of.

B: This is entirely too complex for my mind, yet it does emphasize the need for multiple lives to gain any level of awareness you have shared this evening.

L: I understand that relating this discussion in human terms to be understood is a challenge. It is for both you and me.

B: And just for the record, all soul energy has the capacity to develop the level of awareness about which you are talking.

L: That answer would be yes—even the smallest or youngest of soul energies.

B: Explain for a moment how the chaotic nature of energy relates to positive advancement or soul movement in the octopus' analogy because I am uncertain how to understand what would happen if a soul slips and moves down backward in an incarnation.

L: That happens to all souls, and they are then able to relearn the things that caused the slippage.

B: Are those issues forgotten in the afterlife, or do they need to be reexperienced?

L: Actually, they need to learn how to trust themselves to learn again; it is never forgotten in its entirety. Some souls will try to build walls to avoid slipping. In some ways, you are like that, especially when you get stuck on a question; you do not want to get tripped up and shut down.

B: It is silly for me to say this, but just being aware provides protection. Just that alone would give souls an advantage in avoiding slipping.

L: Again, you would be correct. Do you know that in your world, it is forgiveness that is the hardest thing to do, especially with all the chaos being experienced? Sadly, not having the ability to forgive illustrates an unhealthy self, and a healthy self is required to advance as a soul in the afterlife.

Here is something that ties back to our discussion but relates to what we are talking about regarding chaos. Answer me this: Why is everything in a container?

B: Because it provides for better management or control—the establishing of necessary boundaries?

L: If there were no containers, what would happen? Everything in the container would have the capacity to go rogue, and those environments create a state of fear. Imagine the elements of a human cell going negative and releasing that type of alarm state. Cells in an anxious state attach to anything and begin to lose their purpose.

Now imagine the same thing happening in your afterlife picture with the head of the octopus and the elements in each soul energy coupling with that fear. This discussion answers the original question regarding tornadoes, earthquakes, et cetera.

B: Air, outside its container, attaching itself to everything and anything, all in a state of rogue fear introducing the material for a violent tornado.

What I need to do currently is try to reexplain the concept of the octopus' analogy but with the influence of the basic elements—an integration of sorts. Understanding how everything operates brings the level of awareness necessary to make any appropriate changes.

L: That would be correct. We need to explain that analogy in a precise and detailed fashion. Unfortunately, I need to hold off on that for another time and another writing discussion. For now, it is only required that the soul understand it is part of a small, designed cluster of similar vibrations or energies. They are your true mates, working together within their individualized life incarnations to learn as much as they can about a desired part of life. In your case, it is healing; therefore, you and your mates are experiencing the yin and yang of healing throughout multiple lives. That is the basic and fundamental understanding of the analogy. Obviously, because of what I have inserted here, there is much more to that story, but first I need to have you concentrate on the chaotic energies that affect those learning environments. Everything eventually affects the head of the octopus.

I want to stop now. We will continue next time. I am only asking that you think about the required vessels we have talked about and bring your remaining questions.

At this point in my spiritual journey, asking questions about ley lines, rogue energies, the octopus analogy, and individual human cell development is not a point of moral or ethical importance. They are simply starting points for future narrative contemplation and whether I will continue to experience embarrassing moments when I just do not get where Laz is going. As an example, I am curious as to whether my brief encounter with the discussion of containers and vessels has been squeezed into a form of endless awkwardness for both myself and those who try to digest this latest conversation.

To avoid any continued loss of composure on this matter, here is what I believe. Most of us admit that we are uncomfortable with unorthodox information because our understanding of life has been hardened by how we have been accustomed to judging everything around us. Unfortunately, on many occasions, we get stuck by trying to change these thoughts by simply letting substitute ideas engulf our existing belief systems. Regardless of how this line of thinking advances, becoming wedged in odd, otherworldly situations is a cause for concern for even the most adventurous unearthly traveler.

In thinking about my last comment, I cannot recall ever imagining nature's elements being enclosed in a container, and that includes the idea that my body, in fact, is an identified vessel. Trying to come to terms with the concept that elements reside in an enclosed environment is like struggling to view my face clearly in a shattered mirror— the resulting image is just too muddled and out of focus.

Similarly, after years of spiritual exploration, there are times when I still do not understand how my mind operates. When I try to wrestle with its in-depth workings, I find myself blurred by overlapping thoughts. With this latest discussion, I am nurturing this theory: Am I listening hard enough? And if I'm not, is it possible I may never fully grasp these unorthodox concepts? And if that happens, is it likely that my journey will skip off its rails?

I am curious about the forthcoming discussion on dirt and rocks, and my thinking resembles that of a nervous and hungry young black-bird. I fear that I may find myself hopping from tree to tree.

Chapter 9

Dirt and Rocks

I have been thinking about the moments when life presents unanticipated gifts. Not the ones that are wrapped and bowed on Christmas morning, but the instances when we are presented with unintended learning opportunities. In a way, it is like we have received a type of ESP message—unique intelligent forms of insight that shape novel mental images.

Whenever I encounter an unintended mental state, Laz encourages me to deal with my most immediate sensory conditions. He is especially insistent when assessing mental gifts that appear to come out of nowhere. Regularly, he wraps unexpected events together and talks about how those instances are entries into a deep personal relationship with the universe.

My friend's style of thinking may be difficult to preserve as I try to prepare for a discussion about rocks and dirt—the fundamental components of the earth. And the reasoning behind that? In many ways, my life relationships have been determined exclusively by emotionally focusing on a person or object. Regarding rocks and dirt, I have no life-long meaningful attachment.

What matters, however, is my current belief that unorthodox information involving relationships with inanimate objects is not part of the negative chaos I experience. It can be an obstacle, but it is more likely an opportunity for a deeper level of awareness, but only if I can take the time to challenge my historical thoughts. Fortunately, what is encouraging from my soul companion's stories are the multiple ways he cuts through historical beliefs about nature and develops fresh insight and clarity.

When I asked my friend Khenchen about the diverse tempos I was experiencing in my afterlife journey, he compared it to the Buddhist Sanskrit word *vipashyana*, translated as "to see things in an extraordinary way," not as one would think they are or want to be but as they truly are. Predictably, my monk friend referenced a classic *vipassana* meditation standard he would often repeat to me and paraphrased in this fashion: while examining added information, focus on your personal evaluation of what has been said and remember to use your Buddhist "super seeing."

My soul guide has been taking an unusual path. He has a very compelling topic—the impact of nature's elements. Yet he has failed to show how my afterlife experience may be directly altered. As a result, this spiritual endeavor in the world of souls has become a gut-level experience. Clearly this is not something I can fake my way through, hoping I can arrive at an impressive conclusion to share with others, and that troubles me.

———

Laz: Can you tell me what a rock really is?

Bud: Excuse me?

L: I know that is an odd question, so let me answer it for you. A rock is life.

B: You previously shared that water was life, so how would that be different?

L: And that would be correct. So, what are we talking about here?

We are talking about how all the elements are connected and, in effect, one. If all this is true, teach me how dirt would be life.

B: The only thing I can think of at this moment is that dirt might be the foundation for the other elements to be created or born.

L: You would be correct. It is the foundation, and you always need a place to gather your footing. Without it, there would be no permanence.

B: Tell me this, Laz: In bringing your initial question back to our discussion of the impact of the elements on one's afterlife, how is the human shell analogous to dirt or the foundation of life?

L: Let's get into this. But first, tell me why rocks are here and what they are all about.

B: Could rocks be a foundation storage library of events that have occurred over time? Could the combination of silt, sand, and soil, which make up a rock, contain the history of that rock's existence—what it has been through?

L: You are on to something, so keep going with that thought.

B: Could they be the recorders of the planet's energy over a particular period?

L: Yes, but why?

B: Is it because they are connected to every other element that existed during that period?

L: Now you have it. Imagine this for a moment. The rocks of this earth contain incredible information because they have been the recorders, and yet people climb over them on mountains and have no idea of the history they are stepping on and never absorb or think of it.

B: Laz, you do understand that what you have just stated is clearly odd. I do not know anyone who would begin to consider what you just said to me.

L: I would like to look at this more closely. As an example, look at a diamond and tell me how it was made. Every element had to be involved in the process of making that diamond.

B: I understand, but how does something like this play out in my afterlife experience?

L: Why would it not? You need all the elements to have an afterlife experience because there would be no life or afterlife without them. The shell you occupy is made of these elements.

B: Are you trying to tell me that the awareness of what is contained within a rock is an advantage for me in the afterlife? I have no connection to that way of thinking.

L: It would be more of an advantage if you were aware of all this now in your human life. Here is an example: Why do people buy crystals?

B: I assume simply because they like the features of the crystal.

L: That may be superficially correct, yet there are some who buy them for the energy they receive. A crystal is a rock but with a more advanced energy field.

B: Help me out because this is very confusing. If someone wanted to pursue this train of thought, what would they need to do to access what you are talking about?

L: They would have to know more about the elements than they currently realize. Elements have the capacity to create solid form, and a rock would be an example of that because all the elements are contained in it. Much like you, the rock is from air, water, fire, and the soil of the earth.

B: Let me move closer to the afterlife picture. How does a soul perceive its association with and connection to the elements? As an example, does it see the bigger picture—that everything is tied together?

L: The soul perceives what you are referencing instantly once it enters the afterlife. Why would it not?

B: Is all this planned? In other words, are we expected to experience what it is like to be an element?

L: For many it is expected, but that rarely occurs. The determining factor is the soul's development, its frequency, and its vibration. The higher the force field, the more it is expected.

B: The higher the development, the more a soul would be putting this life puzzle together?

L: Absolutely. The fact that a soul would be unaware of this is an indication of that soul's energy development.

Here is another example to explain some of this. In your world, people who are highly spiritual—specifically, your monks—can concentrate and move themselves into a cocoonlike state of light. Suddenly, they can grasp this concept because, at those moments, they relate to everything, including the basic elements of life.

B: I am confused. How does something like that relate to the elements?

L: They can approach the fundamental levels of energy within each element and, in the process, absorb the characterizations of each one.

B: You will have to excuse me for shaking my head, but I cannot help but think we are treading on strange turf.

L: It only has the appearance of being bizarre to those who are not truly spiritually developed frequencies. Young souls whose energy does not allow them to see things through new eyes.

B: The only way for me to begin to make sense of this is if I can manage to align myself with a theory in which everything is connected. If I can get myself there, some of what you are relating can become a viable option.

L: Maintaining that position would be correct. Everything is connected—your organs, bones, flesh, body, everything.

Now, to make it even more challenging, let us look at the planet as if it were its own element. As a starting point, the planet itself is made up of the basic elements.

If the planet is made of rocks that are laced within the soil and loaded with information, do you think that the shifting of continents might provide the answers that many of you seek? Could that be a mechanism of protecting energies within its makeup of the basic elements?

B: Are you suggesting that the elements of the planet might align in such a manner as to prohibit activities—positive or negative?

L: Yes, and it may be more intense when large bodies of water are involved. Here is an example you might not like to talk about, but it does exist. There is a portion of your oceans that creates very unusual events; why would that be, and why are there so many unanswered questions about this location?

B: Are you referencing the Bermuda Triangle?

L: The answer is a simple spiritual one—that portion of the earth is protecting itself.

Here is an analogy. Presume for a moment that you injure your arm badly, and it hurts. Now it is bandaged, and you as well as others keep touching it. Eventually, you would get to the point when you would put your arm behind your back when you saw someone coming as a means of protection, would you not? You would be intentionally avoiding the pain. In so many words, this is what happens with areas like that.

B: And all this exists because of the makeup of everything?

L: It is all one conscious mind, so your answer is yes.

B: I find this interesting, yet I still have difficulty understanding how something like this plays out in an afterlife scenario.

L: If you are advanced and aware and you pass over, part of what you refer to as a life review cycle includes how you viewed and participated in the planet's events—its storms, its beauty, its evolution. Did you care about any of that? Your review, your personal judgment, will include the world in which you reside.

There is only one way to navigate your planet and that is by being acutely aware of the connectedness of everything.

B: Is it as simple as this: awareness of this is a form of soul evolution?

L: If a soul travels with a cloak of fear, its vibration is lowered, and its afterlife experience is directly affected.

B: Here is a simple question: Are younger souls aware of the responsibility they must take on to intimately align with the basic elements of life?

L: No. What you are suggesting is an advanced soul activity, and something like that would clearly identify an energy that was moving up its evolutionary chain.

B: If a soul were able to identify a mentor or healer, would that assist in positive evolutionary movements?

L: Actually, ley lines are fashioned to do exactly what you are suggesting. They are the veins of the planet, protecting and producing complex energies.

B: I have a thought. Do ley lines act much like the veins in a human body, with everything moving through those positions?

L: Yes. Here is how they connect to your afterlife picture. When you pass over to the other side, those souls associated with a ley line, mentally or otherwise, ascend through the afterlife experience much more quickly than those who are emotionally at a distance. They have a vastly different energy field.

B: Are you suggesting it is an advantage?

L: No. You can interpret it this way: the ley line is like the blood-stream but made of water.

B: It is an input of energy?

L: Yes. It is not an advantage as you suggested. You would not move off your life accomplishments or the lack of them. You would simply be moving at a quicker pace through the afterlife experience I explained to you in *Soul Afterlife: Beyond the Near-Death Experience*. There is a lower percentage chance that the soul would be dragged down by the absence of association with the elements while living. Do you understand?

B: I am assuming it is exclusively an afterlife navigation advantage.

L: You are less likely to get stuck in your review, so your answer is yes. Think of this: imagine you are going through a dark tunnel, and you see a light at the end. Just before you reach it, you feel the wind increase, and suddenly dirt and rocks are pelting you. That is a possibility if you have not been connected prior to passing. It is not an act of punishment; it is the soul suddenly becoming aware of having missed the connection. The soul is telling itself, "Oh! That is right; I missed all that."

B: Is there an advantage at that point?

L: Yes. Becoming aware and not putting on the brakes as it moves through the afterlife. It avoids being stuck and wondering what all this is about—what is going on?

This does not happen often, but imagine being stuck in the element of earth. It would be dark, as if you were walking down a road and losing all the light. Just that alone would create a position where the soul would stop and put on the brakes.

Here is what I consider fascinating: souls who have passed over and had the experience of being temporarily stuck within one or all the elements never return to tell anyone of this challenge. They do, however, note it for future incarnations and, hopefully, retain it so that they avoid those delays in future soul reviews. Regardless of the vibration or frequency of the latest incarnation, the soul has become more "sensitive" to the connection with the elements.

On the positive side of this, there is no concept of time in the spiritual world, so all souls eventually do "get it."

B: I have an odd question before we end this evening. Throughout this discussion, I have wondered whether, if I had an encounter with an element—I was caught in a tornado, trapped in a disastrous fire, or perished in a flood—would I be hypersensitive to that element in my next incarnation?

L: Absolutely. Any event you suggested would be directly attached to your aura. That, coupled with the fact that you are of the elements, would also factor into your answer; everything is connected.

B: To close out this evening, what will we discuss next time?

L: There is a triangle to all the elements, and I would like to share that with you.

Chances are if you are reading or listening to this book, you have a well-developed fascination with what happens in an afterlife experience. For most of us, those beliefs are fixed in traditional philosophical or religious theories.

Here is something I would like you to consider. For just one moment, try to imagine something out of the ordinary. Suppose we were able to study alternative ideas freely and without the constraints of historical convictions. Try to imagine a time when we could investigate current information without ignorance, desire, or aversions. Think about the alternative points of view we would discover.

I would like to believe that when confronted with unorthodox ideas, there are times when everything suddenly becomes a rare blessing. A time when newly formed thoughts become fertile ground through which I discover unique awareness.

Unfortunately, regarding the earth element and the influence of rocks and dirt, I am frankly unable to properly find the way through that process. Philosophical experiments designed to imagine a connection with rocks and dirt may be one thing; realistically identifying a personal relationship that I might have with them will require a radically different mindset.

While piloting this spiritual treasure hunt, I have been told that igneous rocks—rocks for which the element of fire is identified as a process of melting and cooling—eventually break down and erode to form silt (sand). Geologists might point out that the source of fire for a rock is both internal (convection currents) and external (the effects imposed by the sun). Further, air and water are consistently at play throughout the existence of a rock.

All the above may give a rationale for the interplay of nature's elements and begin to present the understandable connectiveness of everything—a soulful journey in which I will be able to account for how the world's elements play out in an afterlife experience. As for a detailed explanation of how that might occur for me personally? I am waiting on that discussion.

Up to this point, I have been receiving only a small sequence of ancient truth-seeking teachings regarding the connection to the afterlife. Going forward, I hope more is in the offing as I move into how the shape of a triangle affects the elements and human afterlife.

Chapter 10

Triangles

Many years ago, I studied the Buddhist concept of mental consciousness—the offbeat philosophy that states that beyond the basic five senses of sight, hearing, smell, taste, and touch, there exists a sixth sense. This sixth sensation is not to be confused with what some might refer to as ESP. Rather, it is analogous to what a cognitive psychologist might describe as the capacity to sort out information through the senses. It references my capacity to discern various energies that influence my life. Regarding the basic elements of nature, it is my ability to form a useful theory or mental images of the world I occupy.

In seeking an exit ramp from these past narratives, historical Buddhist teachings would make my internal debate trouble free. Here is how that might occur: Buddhist philosophy would simply suggest that it would be beneficial for me to experience the basic elements of life through my five senses. If that were realistically possible, then Laz could be viewed as merely sending problematic, life-altering messages in my direction and inviting me to ask more probing questions as my journey continues. At that point in my voyage, his intention has become clear cut: to remove any doubt that exists, I need to find my own answers to the world of nature's elements.

I have never considered terminating this voyage prematurely; however, I have persistent internal questions that occupy my thinking. Here are several examples: What is this otherworldly experience teaching me? Am I seeing my soul guide's intentions clearly? Why do I almost immediately see his ideas and messages as blurry and indistinct? Can the thoughts about my association with nature's elements become diluted over time?

No matter what may be forthcoming, my obligation is to observe the fundamental connection I have with nature's elements. In many ways, it would be familiar, like the way my thoughts often change as I lose myself while watching a rushing waterfall. At those moments, my intention is to become a sentinel, to see if my relationship with what I am witnessing changes over time.

With the upcoming discussion of nature's triangles, Laz once shared how air connects to the conscious and unconscious. Can that really be the type of triangles he is referencing?

———————

Laz: Let us get started because I want to give you something to think about before I give you a clear connection to the afterlife. I would like you to tell me what you see when you look at the pyramids. They are triangles, correct?

Bud: Yes. Are you suggesting something else?

L: Assume that you could take two triangles and place them on top of each other with the tips facing in different directions. What would that be? What would that create?

B: On top of each other but facing in different directions?

L: Exactly. Let me help. It would look like a Star of David, but that is not where we are going this evening.

Here is something else: I would like you to stand up for just one moment and think of the triangle that is on you—shoulders wide and filtering down to your feet. You have an upside-down triangle; your body is designed that way.

Now, what do they have in common—the pyramids and your body design—and how might that affect the elements that we have been talking about all this time?

B: Does it have something to do with the flow of energy?

L: You're close with that comment. Let me help again. It represents the spark of life. That might answer why there are so many of those structure types all over your world. Many ancient people knew of this and the connection it manifested. It is a correspondence and a spark of life.

B: Is it a requirement for creation?

L: It is just part of it. And part of a very deep rabbit hole that we will not touch during our discussion regarding the association with the elements tonight.

But let me take you closer to how this relates to the elements directly. All the elements operate within the confines of a triangle because that image connects directly to you.

For a moment, go back to the octopus analogy. Think of the triangle on the octopus within the analogy. If it were standing right side up, what would you see?

B: The head of the octopus would be like the tip of the pyramid, and the base would represent all life's incarnations falling out of the head of the octopus.

L: Now place that imaginary octopus upside down—what do you see?

B: The opposite of what I just explained.

L: The biggest part of the triangle is where the weight of the triangle sits—that really represents the brain, the power, the logic—but sadly enough, the point represents all that filtering out and leaving you —draining itself.

Think now of the triangle being used in every element in both examples we have just discussed—right sided and upside down.

B: Yin and yang?

L: Yes, represented by the triangle. What you are learning tonight is intended to be focused on what you need to do if your human or spiritual information is filtering out while upside down. And what strategies need to be deployed to reverse that flow.

Let me give you some assistance here. The ancients knew of this, which is why the pyramids are facing upward with the desire of the information of the universe filtering down and inward to the base of knowledge, stored for all time.

Now, if you have both triangles on you at once—point up and point down—that is when you have the optimum balance in life. That is your answer for the phrase *as above, so below.*

Most people have the triangles separated, like when you look in a mirror. You see yourself, but what is seeing you?

B: Interesting.

L: Now let's talk about the elements. Every one of them has a triangle. Unless it can match itself—triangle on top of another triangle for balance—which is not occurring at this time. That is why you are now experiencing extreme forms of weather. Couple that with the absence of balance within the people of your planet, and you can quickly have a real mess on your hands. If you could align nature's triangles and human triangles, that would be the desired balance and, as a result, the ultimate power of the elements.

B: And you are talking about balance on all four of the basic elements, correct?

L: Yes, that is correct. Here is where I wish to go with this discussion. Tell me, please, what encourages the lack of balance we just discussed?

B: Is human chaos at the heart of this balancing problem?

L: If so, what would be four or five reasons for the out-of-balance problem?

B: I am guessing, but let's try these as answers: ignorance, following the crowd and caving in on what you honestly believe, internal fear, feeling trapped, and becoming a victim.

L: With sharing these, could they also be the reason your triangle is not balanced?

B: You can assume that, yes.

L: If so, then how can you balance all that out? If you honestly believe these are the reasons for disequilibrium, what are your solutions?

B: One would be to find a way to increase one's self-esteem and reduce the need for continued validation.

L: And if that is absent, why would you be in that state? The problem is not being dealt with. There is no awareness.

B: I am having a challenge with this portion of our discussion.

L: Frankly, it is the only way for me to show you how out of balance everything is in your world. I am not picking on you personally.

B: The actual answer is that the only control I have is to deal with my own personal environment and subsequently that would apply to everyone.

L: Correct. And here is the advantage of that: once your environment is adjusted, things around you are adjusted as well. That is how real change happens. Think like a Human Warrior—one who does not cave in when standing in a crowd of one thousand people who believe differently.

All this is intended to go back to the basics and to show you how your condition directly affects everything that surrounds you. It is all an intimate and deeply personal direct connection. Here is an example. Look at water for one moment. What would be four things that would make the water around you out of balance?

B: My first thought is abuse. Second, how we think or do not think about the connection to water; we ignore any direct association. How the vibration of water would become more chaotic from all this, and its energy would become displaced. This may be repetitive, but I cannot rid myself of the thought of abandonment—a complete lack of interest.

L: The abandonment is the most critical one you have mentioned, and the irony of that statement is how much of all of you is made up of water.

Would you believe me if I suggested that with abandonment, there would be a sense of anger, a displacement of intention by water? Does it make sense that if you are abandoned, an alternative reaction would be to do the same in return? What would occur if water started to abandon all of you?

The element of water has an extremely specific job. It is to keep you and everything else alive, and although it does not think like a human, its energy field does modify itself based on what it is picking up from what is around it—really, in an offbeat way, it is no different from how your vibration becomes adjusted.

Think about how amazing it would be if all of you could connect to the water and come back to the water. Especially regarding how to appreciate water. Realizing that water is an integral part of everything and that you are made up of mostly water. All that would give the element of water the balance I am suggesting is missing. Once that happens, everything else regarding water would balance out—especially all of you.

B: If we could balance just one element, would that assist in having the others balanced as well?

L: Absolutely. In fact, it would be a domino effect you would see.

So, now that we have talked about water, let us examine at the element of fire. Looking at fire the same way as we did water, what would be a few things that would place fire out of balance?

B: Being used for inappropriate purposes, not as intended. Not being aligned with the fire of human shells, no connection.

L: How about when fire is not an intentional thought and viewed only as harmful? Not considering the positive and helpful portions of fire that relate to cooking, heating and, well, as the internal fire within all humans. Here is something you never think about: there is an internal fire within your belly that processes everything injected into your body; it is what keeps you going. There is no acknowledgment, it is never really thanked by anyone, and it is only noticed when it bites back. Currently, it is out of balance.

If it were possible to balance the triangle of fire, it would have to come with a desire to show respect.

B: How do any of us get over the view that fire is harmful?

L: Ironically, that is necessary. Most people only see and think of fire when it is raging and burning everything down. Yet fire is electricity, it is heating homes, it is your sun and keeps everything going. Without fire there is no light, no growth, no plants; nothing survives. It delivers essential nutrients to all people.

What do you think the intention of a solar flare is? Science would certainly have one answer to that question, but is it possible that there are other answers as well? That it is an act of abandonment of connection?

I find it interesting that in your ancient times, there was a continual effort to thank the sun for its assistance, but who does that now? It seems to me that everyone complains if it is too hot. Again, this is the type of instability that produces an abusive state, and the fire of the sun, in this case, simply reacts.

The point I am trying to make in the discussion of fire is this: it is about acknowledgment and appreciation.

B: Are you suggesting that unanticipated acts by fire are a way of saying "Pay attention to me"?

L: Of course. To move on—let us talk about earth. This gets more complex because you are on the earth.

Like before, what do you think might be upsetting the earth because there is an absence of balance?

B: I believe that many of the comments I have would be identical to what we just talked about. Here is one difference: the earth gives us so much, yet we intentionally cover it up or, worse, bury our trash in it.

L: You are right on that point, and what might be sadder is that the people who know what you just said will not publicly acknowledge that imbalance. Here is an example: people who walk down the street and step over a piece of garbage, never stopping to think whether the planet wants it there.

Additionally, nothing good can come from burning the earth or from covering up the earth to create a road. I know they are necessary, but there is an absence of attention to how it affects the earth's balance.

Here is a learning for you: the absence of balance creates chaos, which then mixes with the chaos of the people around it. Digging, blacktopping, leveling trees, and destroying natural resources and minerals for the human shell to survive represents an absence of awareness or intention to balance out what has been done. All this shows a lack of respect.

Is it possible that actions as we have just described can make the earth—or anyone, for that matter—angry? Can that anger mix with the lack of balance and create the environment for earthquakes, landslides, et cetera? Can that be the earth's way of saying, "I am here, and stop what you are doing"?

Eventually, these conditions can be amplified to create a shift within the earth because only a few are taking this seriously. It would be like a dog shaking fleas off its back.

B: You may not want to share this with me, but has something like that happened before?

L: Within the history of all things human? Many times, by modifying the equator and shifting the poles, just to mention two ways that can manifest.

Ironically, if there was a serious sense of balance, you would see the elements join and eliminate the fluctuations in weather that trouble your earth. Imagine having springlike weather all year around. Food sources would multiply while everything was thriving and connecting.

Simply put, the earth is the biggest connection of all the elements because it works directly with the intent to secure human survival, yet it is not acknowledged for those efforts.

B: Talk about air for a moment.

L: Again, what would be your suggested cause for an imbalance?

B: My obvious first response is that we purposely infest it with pollution. What makes that my number one item is the irony that once polluted, we breathe it in and contaminate ourselves.

L: Think of it this way for just one spiritual moment: Can that be air's way of getting back at those who poisoned it? Your gifts for polluting air are pulmonary illness, lung cancers, sinus issues, breathing issues, and, finally, brain problems.

B: I believe my only other major issue for air would be the disassociation with the element despite its level of importance, taking it for granted.

L: Can you see how most of what you share is repetitive? Can that be by design? Do you simply assume that they exist for your pleasure? That is such a wrong assumption.

The connection that is required by people is identical to the connection that trees, plants, and animals have with all four elements. The absence of that is your major problem while living, never mind what that imbalance creates once you are in your afterlife, which is magnified threefold.

Bud, before we adjourn, what do you think the result of this imbalance creates? I am curious about how you see all this.

B: I cannot shake the thought that most of our disease is magnified from all this, if not actually created by it.

L: You would be correct.

B: One last comment: last time, you talked about the triangle of air. The connection between breath, consciousness, and unconsciousness. That all three are happening at the same time. Did you want to speak about that?

L: All the elements work that way. The absence of an intimate understanding of the triangle connection between you and the elements fuels the imbalance of all four.

B: Laz, connect this discussion to the afterlife for just a moment.

L: Think about this: if someone dies, and their energy and/or vibration is not balanced, what do you think happens to them? Not only does it lower their total energy field, but it also pushes down that soul's growth and development.

With balance, there is a stabilization of most of the soul's energy; with the absence of balance, the soul often is required to start all over and learn and experience everything we have just discussed. The soul is absent the energy necessary to stabilize itself.

B: Let me try a human analogy to understand this afterlife connection. Assume that we all operate on a scale from zero to ten, with ten being the highest. I have lived a life of a seven, but the association with the elements has been minimal, at a level three. How does a soul move through the afterlife in that situation?

L: Sadly, you would be brought down closer to a level three. Remember, it is all about vibration. The three would adjust your vibration and, subsequently, your soul's energy. The higher the vibration, the better off and quicker the life review journey will be that we discussed in *Soul Afterlife*.

B: This is a revelation for me because it is a much broader discussion than just the elements and a focus on balancing out the life experience in total.

L: Yes. So many souls are stuck in a loop because of what we have talked about this evening. This results in incarnations that do not move with a vertical trajectory but repeat one similar life after another.

On the positive side, there is no time limit for a soul to acquire what we have discussed. Eventually, all souls do move on. But do not take what we have discussed here lightly. The loop just referenced is a serious challenge for all souls.

For a moment, go back and reconsider our talk about spiritual empathy. That is what is required. As a soul, you would not want to be caught trying to reconcile problems with the vibration of three-sided structures: triangles.

B: For the record, if a soul happens to be caught, does it know that it must address the triangle of the elements in its next incarnation?

L: As with all things, it knows before incarnating yet needs to find the direct association once it starts its new life. There is so much that interferes with a direct relearning assignment.

Here is something we will talk about another time, but it relates to tonight's discussion and, specifically, the vibration of the three-sided triangle. As we said in the beginning, placing one triangle on top of another upside down and creating the image of one triangle lying on top of another in reverse position is analogous to placing two number threes face to face. Now, having done that, what do you have?

B: You would have created the number eight. Correct?

L: And what is that? Look closely because it also represents the continuation of life.

We have traveled as far as I would like regarding the elements of nature and the human association that is required. Next time, I would like to write the conclusion of this debate and specifically address the direct connection to the afterlife experience. That puzzle is often complex, yet it can be navigated with the simple skill of awareness.

Throughout this journey, there has been one special learning I would like to share. I have come to know that the gradual process of disclosing unusual spiritual information is not an obstacle but an opportunity to discover deeper levels of awareness. If I rejected this way of thinking, it is likely that my ability to provide insight would be stymied, and the possibility of balancing out any life triangles would be out of the question.

I mentioned that my Buddhist friend Khenchen once referred to the process of gaining insight as one's ability to gain super seeing. He would frequently remind me that right understanding was an intuitive, gut-level practice, like feeling your way through a darkened room to find a door that might open. How during every blind step taken, you ask whether the exit path chosen is direct and capable of allowing for exceptional decisions.

Tonight's triangle of life discussions has placed me in an awkward position. Several days after this debate, while fixating on the impact of nature's elements, I found myself suddenly alarmed in the middle of the night. For a second or two, I was disoriented, and it was impossible for me to attach one single thought to the reality of the moment. To my advantage, eventually those distorted times resulted in clearing a path toward moments when I would begin to think more clearly. For example, "OK, that is what Laz was intending to teach about connectiveness."

With the unconventional subject of afterlife soul activity and messages regarding how I am personally out of balance as my backdrop, I should not be surprised to find myself detached from nature's elements. Let me explain that comment further. There is a subtle sense of disparity or separation that lies at the heart of how I have abandoned the basic elements of nature. And the absence of any form of healthy connectiveness simply adds to the problem.

To settle any confusion concerning nature's spark of life, Laz suggests I develop a spiritual form of empathy. He is encouraging me to construct a clear understanding by which I can accept whatever difficulty I may experience in recognizing how I might have abandoned any connection to nature.

At the end of the day, this is what I hope for: the ability to create an environment of uplifting compassion toward the basic elements of life. Hopefully, that will gradually open a profound experience of fearlessness. A time when courage can transform personal imbalance into a strong motivation to align with nature's unique and intended abilities. If such an act is successful, I may be capable of understanding my true intimate association with water, air, fire, and earth.

Next, Laz intends to write the conclusion to *The Afterlife Experience*. I have asked only that he speak directly to how the awareness of what he has shared contributes to what I might experience after passing.

Chapter 11

Conclusion

As previously mentioned, Laz was insistent on writing the conclusion to our discussion about the afterlife experience. He was equally firm that it be a deeply personal learning session, not simply a narrative by him on what we had covered throughout these many weeks. He further stated that from his viewpoint and as my personal guide, it is important for me to understand how this information has a real-time effect on my current life. The following represents his thoughts verbatim.

Laz: I have several questions for you tonight. Let me start with this: How many people do you feel are grateful for what they have? Moreover, if they are not grateful, could that lead to problems with the afterlife mysteries we have been discussing recently? As an example, could there be increasing problems with the air they breathe? Could the same be said for water, fire, and the amazing planet they stand on? At this stage of our discussion, I might suggest to you that until they can evaluate the connection we have been debating, it is virtually impossible for them to become thankful and evaluate their happiness upon passing.

When examining the afterlife picture, individuals need a direct association with nature's elements to move forward with an assessment of their soul's earthly accomplishments and, subsequently, the entirety of an afterlife journey.

Here is something that is never openly taught or discussed. Upon entering an afterlife process, the first mysteries a soul faces are whether it had a direct fellowship with nature's four basic elements. The reason behind that statement? It is because the elements of nature are imbedded within the human experience. Just having them available and enjoyed during a life experience is not the spiritual description of a profound relationship.

Consider this for a moment: if a soul were fortunate enough to have an in-depth association with any of the elements, a heightened burst of energy would be experienced immediately upon passing. This type of energy linking increases all aspects of a soul incarnation experience and, as a result, the afterlife experience as well. Here is an amazingly simple example to explain what I mean. If, during your most recent incarnation, you were a healer and helped the poor better manage their lives, the positive excitement regarding that experience would be amplified tenfold simply by having an additional connection to all life's natural elements. The elements that make up both parties would be positively activated because both are made of those ingredients.

On the other side of the debate, if there was an absence of connection to nature's basic elements, the fitting together of life events would become clouded and the soul's learning diminished. The net results: despite the positive life attention to helping the poor, that soul obstructed its immediate advancement. That incarnation would lack the energy boost I am sharing with you.

Bud: If all this is true, how much weight is given to my relationship to the elements when compared to all the life experiences my soul would confront in an afterlife?

L: Everything is weighed and, as I have suggested, will be exaggerated depending on the level connection, including your comprehensive "live review."

Try to remember this as you evaluate your position prior to passing when you are out of your human shell: everything is significantly amplified. Here are some simple examples. If you liked someone, those feelings would be increased and the same if you did not like someone. All your energy is magnified.

Here is another way to look at this: the human shell acts like an incredible grounder, and there is a reason for that. Your human body grounds you to the element of the earth, but once you are out of your shell, that attachment is no longer present. Everything is enhanced, and your soul is in a free-fall position. In so many ways, the act of breaking down the grounding effect immediately enlarges everything surrounding the soul.

B: It is important for me to clearly understand your comments tonight. The soul progresses through all the stages of an afterlife you represented in *Soul Afterlife: Beyond the Near-Death Experience*, and as you move through the "layers" of an afterlife, the soul is specifically influenced by how I dealt with the elements of life?

L: Try to think of it this way. Imagine that each of the elements is a living energy. Assume also that you abused them or used them for an undesirable purpose. You would experience the negativity associated with having taken those actions. It would be like the example I gave you in other writings, when your human actions may have hurt someone in the schoolyard, and now in the afterlife, you are the one feeling the punches.

Here is something else for your notebook: ascending nonphysical souls realize that the elements are represented in each of the chakras. Further, those souls see and feel the troubles and excitement that an association with the nature's components brings. They acutely identify with earth's components as they move through an incarnation review and deeply into the afterlife.

On the other hand, here is what many young souls experience: the absence of an understanding of how they are intimately connected to earth's fundamental elements becomes an immediate shock upon passing. They become instantaneously aware of how they have always been made of the elements but never drew a meaningful personal line to connect. In an odd manner, they become momentarily paralyzed. Here is the bottom line, and I hope I have made this abundantly clear over the past several months: you are of the elements, which is why they are part of your review in an afterlife, and that is why the impact can be dramatic.

B: To understand this in more detail, upon passing, I am critiquing my incarnation through the lens of my total life experience, including my interactions and association with the elements of life?

L: That is correct. Remember, you are not just evaluating yourself; others are involved as well—you are not the only judge.

B: The elements are involved?

L: In a spiritual way, absolutely. Do not get lost in all this—a life review is comprehensive. Use your super seeing to try and understand that everything is looked at in your afterlife journey. How else would a soul learn or adjust itself for future incarnations?

Let me take you on a brief education journey to help you better understand by asking you this question. I would like to see how much you have learned over all these years.

I believe we have agreed on this: all the elements are deeply fixed in an earthly incarnation, correct? Additionally, I have shared that the elements are part of your soul: your ethereal self, your true self. Finally, as I just stated, all the elements are attached to each component of your chakra energy field. Now, answer me this: If all this is true, what would these elements be?

B: I am trying to understand where you are going with that question.

L: I will state it again. If all the elements are in you, you are in all the elements, and all the elements are in each chakra of the human shell—your energy field—what would the elements be?

B: I am going to take a wild guess—would they be the blueprint for creation?

L: Yes. They are representative of creation, but they are also, by design, an expression of the creator because everything is connected and of the creator.

B: Yet we do not think of the elements in that fashion.

L: I am surprised at that comment. Without any one of the basic elements, all of you would not exist. The elements are what keep all of you alive. To think anything to the contrary would be extremely sad.

B: It would be helpful if you could explain how I would experience a detachment from the elements in the afterlife.

L: You would experience the absence of connection because you are unable to see anything unless you feel it. As an example, you might have to experience what it would be like not to have an earth under your feet, especially if you have avoided any attention to the element of earth while living.

Here is a better example. Imagine that you were part of an industry complex that haphazardly participated in consciously polluting the air —you might experience what it is like not to be able to breathe. The soul undergoes whatever the elements have experienced—positive and negative. That is how all souls learn.

Let me deviate to a related point for just one moment. Assume that you are a believer in the chakra levels of the human body. Suddenly, one specific chakra level becomes unsettled. It is very possible that one of the basic elements of nature has caused that disorder, and your body is responding in an alarm state. Let me give you one more example to emphasize this interaction. Imagine that your solar plexus chakra, your stomach, has been disrupted; why would that be? From a spiritual perspective, the solar plexus represents both the sun and fire. Is it possible that one's attention to that element has slipped off the rails? Could it be possible that your energy field is reacting to a disconnection with the elements I just referenced?

B: Again, this is difficult to follow, but every one of the elements is examined in each of the chakra levels during my existing life and in an afterlife—is that accurate?

L: Yes. Depending on which direction you travel, the connection can be deep and complex. If someone has a heart complication, then the heart chakra is disrupted. If the heart chakra's color is a shade of green, it represents the element of earth and that connection and is positive. But when a heart breaks and sad emotions develop, the color changes according to the emotional and physical attachments that are associated. In a case like that, can you imagine how the elements of nature are likely to respond?

B: Let me bring this back to my level of reality. How does a person's age play into this type of disruption? We are really talking about how human physiology responds.

L: Age is a concept made by the human population. The human shell was designed to be sturdy and to avoid becoming "sick." Your aura is the connection you have to the spirit realm—you are a multidimensional being existing in a shell that you have created, and as a result, any problems that exist, you have created. Your chakra levels are simply representing what you have fashioned.

Bud, we have covered the integration of life's basic workings and how they affect the soul's afterlife experience. Regarding that matter, it is painfully obvious how exceptionally odd that might appear to many. I have shared in the past that, upon passing, most people are concerned with what aligns with their current belief patterns. That is understandable. People seek comfort and emotional shelter whenever the topic of death and an apparent afterlife is introduced. Proposing unconventional options of what occurs after an incarnation terminates can be disquieting. It is my hope, however, that by introducing information intended to modestly encourage awareness, you can consider what might exist beyond what is obvious.

Here is where I would like to end for tonight. Human incarnations and eternal soul existences are magical. To think of a spiritual continuation as occupying a straight line of evolution and growth would be faulty and unproductive. All creation was conceived to be integrated, interlocked, and complex. Is it any wonder that the purpose of a soul's existence has yet to be explained for everyone's satisfaction?

My final comment is this: during the time we have spent together, I have had one objective—for you to understand that the basic components of water, fire, air, and earth are comprehensively tied to your soul growth, and they are deeply part of your afterlife voyage.

Laz has offered an interesting and edgy ending to *The Afterlife Experience: How Our Association with Nature's Elements Shapes the Outcome.* Unfortunately, his thoughts have developed a series of complex and unconventional positions for me personally—specifically in understanding the ongoing stages of a next-world adventure.

Repeatedly throughout my spiritual adventures, I have been asked to look beyond the obvious. It is a phrase that has plagued my thoughts because it is not how unadventurous ideas evolve into my mainstream thinking.

As a result, and prior to starting my review of this year-long debate, I telephoned my Buddhist friend Khenchen. I wanted his advice on my current state of mind. True to form, he listened patiently and promised to get back to me following his weekend retreat. Unexpectedly, the following evening, I received a text message that contained a historical Buddhist story. I recall it this way: an adventurous and wealthy gentleman, while crossing a muddy field, accidently dropped a nugget of gold he was carrying. Over time, the field became a convenient place for local villagers to dump their garbage. The entire area developed into a muddy field of waste. The nugget lay there for centuries, covered by mounds of filth and garbage. Suddenly, a poor villager seeking evidence of the nugget received a message from a higher power encouraging him to look deep within the muck and grime. He was instructed to dig deeply, and once he uncovered the nugget; he was instructed to make something useful out of it. He was not to let his efforts, or the precious nugget, go to waste.

Over time, I have noticed that Khenchen's teaching and advice on serious personal matters often take the form of an analogy. With this electronic notice, the recognition of my internal debate regarding "beyond the obvious" was being obscured by his mud comparison and fueling my confusion and ignorance.

Later, while speaking directly with my monk friend, he shared that using the analogy of the gold nugget seemed to be the easiest path to understanding the confusion brought on by my soulful adventure. He suggested that my answer resided in one question: "What is meant by the gold nugget—or in your case, the words beyond the obvious? Scrape the mud from your thinking, and you are likely to uncover your answer."

In the end, my answers were extremely varied and very reasonable. My world universally resides in what I see, touch, hear, smell, or have come to understand and accept. Outside those historical realities lie only adventurous responses to what may exist and, in real life, become possible.

As an example, is there a difference between the gold nugget and the debated items that Laz has shared? If the mud is withdrawn, the answer might be no. Lifetimes of everyday filth cannot change the nature of gold any more than emotional or mental disturbances can alter my essential nature of exploring new alternative information, unusual as that may be. But just as a thick coat of garbage can camouflage a golden nugget, misunderstandings and old established attitudes can conceal my way of thinking toward everything that encircles life. Any force that obstructs my ability to become open-minded on alternative afterlife options only results in obstructed awareness.

Exploring the world of souls has been a challenge for me. Additionally, it has been a slow, gradual process. Like other spiritual adventures, it takes time to adjust to uncomfortable abstract ideas. Incorporating any eccentric ideas regarding an afterlife experience that is outside the bounds of my understanding confronts all historical dogmatic explanations. I can only presume that understanding how I am directly attached to the basic elements in an afterlife process would fit that image.

Sadly, I have not arrived at definitive answers for readers concerning the realities of an afterlife experience. As I have written, there is only the information that I received from a distant spiritual proxy. Like so many others regarding an afterlife experience, I try to imagine something that brings comfort and peace to my mind. What I do believe, however, is that a mind open to alternative views is a prerequisite to the possible solutions of an afterlife experience. Additionally, it may also assist in removing any faulty beliefs that remain, both now and once I have passed on.

In his "Compensation" essay, Ralph Waldo Emerson discusses the balancing of the forces within the universe, not through physics but through our souls. He insists that there is always some leveling circumstance. Going further, he suggests that life's justice is never permanently delayed. That a perfect level of honesty modifies its balance in every part of life. If Emerson is accurate, the positions taken by my soulful friend might fall in line with his thinking.

Here are my final observations. There were many comments throughout this journey that required moments of attentive meditative calm. At the top of my list is the connection between who I am, the elements of the universe, and the blueprint of a creator's plan. If everything I have been exposed to is accurate, then the connection to nature's elements proposed by Laz just may be intentional by its design. As Emerson stated, "*Oi chusoi Dios aei enpiptousi*—the dice of God are always loaded."

Appendix A
The Human Warrior

Human Warriors are the advancing souls who have their eyes on the horizon, leveling out the good and the bad, and always moving toward a better future. They are not absent from traditional life expectations yet understand that without emotional balance, the best intended life goals can quickly turn and become obstacles to the purpose of one's existence.

Warriors are life-soothing gifts that remind us that we belong to something that is bigger than ourselves. They teach us that incarnations are ancient and never meaningless; that we need to address the building blocks that are required for untried opportunities—the events that circumvent life's difficulties. As an example: most battles chosen by Warriors focus on restoring the positive energy required to keep us on track. And while they work to stabilize life's strengths, we can navigate our anxieties and imperfections.

In the end, Human Warriors are focused, forward-moving souls who never succumb to negative environmental pressures. Rather, they are determined not to become frozen by fear and doubt. Unlike novice souls, a Human Warrior's glass is never half-empty.

Additional References

- "Soul Mechanics – Unlocking the Human Warrior," Bud Megargee, 2017
- budmegargee.com/2021/05/where-have-the-human-warriors-gone

Appendix B
The Octopus Analogy

Souls are dynamic and complex energy fields that gravitate toward similar vibrations and frequencies within the afterlife realm. Due to the amount of diverse energy that exists in the world of souls, naturally aligned soul energies find one another and bond into groups. These cluster group members support each other while forming a core energy unit. This is the beginning of the octopus analogy.

The aligned soul energies shape into what is explained within the analogy as the "head of the octopus." While remaining separate, soul energies develop "learning modules," or designed incarnations, that focus on planned evolutionary themes within the group—for example, becoming healers, artist, teachers, et cetera. The world of souls refers to these joined energies as our "true soulmates." These connected souls have the resource access to several advancing energies but only one primary guide who watches over that soul's development.

Once settled within the head of the octopus, souls have the capacity to split and reassign portions of their energy. That process is like the faceting within a diamond. Anticipating life excursions, a soul assigns a small amount of energy to remain in the head of the octopus, in effect constructing what some refer to as the "higher self." The balance of remaining energy is relegated to the soul's first incarnation.

At this point within the analogy, the soul drops its first octopus tentacle and all the relegated energy travels to the farthest tip of that tentacle, and the first human life plan is initiated. Novice souls are asked to dispense a vast amount of energy to their first incarnation to maximize positive outcomes. What is not planned, but anticipated, are the effects of environmental influences associated with an incarnation —the lifelong, and at times chaotic, variables that every soul is required to navigate.

Successful soul movement within an octopus appendage allows a soul energy to move up the initial appendage through several "multiple lives." During those lifetimes, each individual soul is absorbing every-thing associated with its learning theme—both the yin and yang, the positive and negative. As an example, while seeking to become a healer, the soul would experience being both a doctor and a patient as it moves up a tentacle. In addition, souls would experience variabilities within each life cycle—becoming a different sex, race, accepting challenged mental abilities, or physical handicaps.

In an instance where both positive and negative outcomes are antic-ipated or required, and the novice soul has successfully progressed up its initial appendage, its energy can choose to divide once more. Multiple octopuses' appendages can be considered, each representing a unique incarnation. This act expands the scope of the learning theme. In effect, the soul energy is being asked to accomplish more within its learning module with less energy. These souls have developed the spiri-tual awareness to evolve.

There is no concept of time in the world of souls, therefore multiple incarnations can be initiated within any understood historical timeline, location, or dimension. An advancing soul in the afterlife recognizes every available option, including making the choice to repeat its most recent human life.

Laz has indicated that many of us are young souls working our way through multiple incarnations—or numerous tentacles. As a result, we sense that we are an "old" soul that has, on occasion, experienced portions of a previous life. What is highlighted in the analogy, however, is this: as we work through our "life plans," we are moving up or down our dropped tentacles, and our vibration and frequency changes. Familiarity with these issues would accommodate the feeling of déjà vu that some of us experience. Further, there may be occasions where we have "stalled" within an appendage due to the influence of earthly environmental or dogmatic issues. In that instance, the soul is "looping," or repeating the same life experience and not advancing within the appendage—and moving backward.

Everything explained above is intended to be only the beginning primer for understanding the complex story of the octopus analogy. There is much more to be explained. Additional information can be found in *Soul Afterlife: Beyond the Near-Death Experience*, which builds on what is presented, or by visiting budmegargee.com/blog.

About the Author

Bud Megargee is a former senior health-care executive; a Washington, DC, health-care lobbyist; and an independently published, award-winning author. He began writing after exploring Eastern philosophy and alternative medicine techniques in the professional treatment of emotional challenges at a Taiwanese Buddhist monastery.

Megargee has served as the CEO of the Megargee Healthcare Group LLC, specializing in developing behavioral health medical integration and transformation strategies, and is now living in the beautiful green countryside of southeastern Pennsylvania.

You can visit Megargee at budmegargee.com.

About the Oracle

Shirlet Enama was born in California and has quietly retained a small, exclusive psychic/oracle practice in the rural mountainous region of Berwick, Pennsylvania. She attracted the attention of a Buddhist monastery at an early age, and monks who considered her a child of light encouraged her ability to recognize and openly communicate with otherworldly energies, irrespective of their vibration level or dimension of origin. Regarded as a seer by her unearthly partners, she channels personal soul guides in a comfortable and conventional manner and instructs that the explanations shared are the measured moments of one's life voyage, not a forecast of events to come.

In the role of a practitioner of spiritual voice channeling, Shirlet sits quietly when engaged in casual conversation. There is a gentle and simple calmness to the way in which she presents herself, and that stillness carries over while she's channeling spirit voices from the other side.

For instance, while engaged in spirit-channeling dialogue, there is only a slight noticeable change in voice inflection as she rapidly repeats what is exchanged between her and the channeled spirit. She often describes this as a high-speed computer connection.

For more information about Shirlet and her private practice, visit www.Shirlet.com.

Made in the USA
Middletown, DE
15 September 2022

73152079R00080